Foreword

Pastor James LaFavor and Dr. Trahern LaFavor offer a father and son's perspective on rebuilding and repairing relationships in this book. Both authors are pastors, and both authors have formal training in mental health and spiritual counseling. I highly recommend this book because it is an incredible blueprint and tool for the reader for several reasons. First and foremost, this book is straight from the heart and is somewhat mini-biographical. The authors walk us through their history, their relationship challenges, their understanding of their challenges, and the strategies (e.g., psychological and spiritual) they used to address their relationship challenges. For example, Pastor James LaFavor discusses relationship challenges related to growing up in poverty in Georgia to become a successful pastor, husband, and father in South Florida. Dr. Trahern LaFavor discusses relationship challenges related to rebuilding his life following his playing days in the National Football League (NFL) to receive a Ph.D. and become a Marriage and Family Therapist.

The two authors understand the challenges of relationships and offer the reader a blueprint to address our own relationship challenges. Second and equally as powerful, the authors encourage us not to give up when we encounter relationship challenges, even when we have challenges that seem to present overwhelming odds against us. In a world where people have often given up on relationships too soon, the two authors encourage us and guide us not to give up. They provide us with needed strategies to understand and to address relationship challenges. This book reflects the teaching of Jesus on not giving up. Jesus said, "With God all things are possible." This book calls us to remember the words of Winston Churchill: "Never give in. Never give in."

It also echoes the words of Dr. M. Scott Peck's book, *The Road Less Traveled*. The opening page of this seminal book tells us life is difficult and encourages us to take on the challenges of life. That is, take the road less traveled. Finally, this book reminds me of my grandfather's words. He was a pastor who told his family that at times we may get weary, exhausted, and give out. But refresh yourself and don't give up. Like my grandfather providing me with words of wisdom, Dr. Trahern LaFavor has received words of wisdom from his father. Pastor James LaFavor told Dr. Trahern LaFavor that when life is tough, grab the bull by the horns. Dr. Trahern LaFavor later understood what his father meant:

tough situations do not last, but tough people do. With this book, the reader will learn to become tough during challenging relationship situations, and the reader will learn to overcome their relationship challenges.

Jeff Randall, Ph.D.
Clinical Psychologist
Assistant Professor,
Medical University of South Carolina

Meet the Authors

Pastor James LaFavor is the Senior Pastor of the Universal Christian Church of Christ (UCCOC) in Fort Lauderdale, Florida. He is the founder of UCCOC and for over forty-four years has been serving families in the faith-based community. He is also a Christian Counselor holding a master's degree in Christian Counseling from South Florida Bible and Theological Seminary. Pastor LaFavor also worked as a chaplain and rehabilitation counselor for South Florida Hospital for over seventeen years, where he worked with clients struggling with severe mental health challenges. Pastor LaFavor and the love of his life, Ellaree, who passed in 2018, have five children, including his son Trahern, the co-author of this book. I believe this book will be a practical guide to helping individuals handle relationship challenges.

Trahern LaFavor, Ph.D., has worked with his father in the ministry for over twenty years. Trahern played professional football for the Chicago Bears, Carolina Panthers, Dallas Cowboys, and Baltimore Ravens. After leaving the NFL, he went on to complete his Ph.D. in marriage and family therapy. He also worked as the team clinician for the Miami Dolphins for five years and assisted countless NFL players.

Today, as a licensed minister, Dr. LaFavor brings his vision for a brighter future to today's youth, based largely on his own upbringing and connections with the church. He also works to improve the lives of abused and neglected children.

Pastor LaFavor and Dr. LaFavor reside in Fort Lauderdale, Florida.

Dedication

In loving memory of my dear wife, Ellaree LaFavor, who inspired me to pursue our dreams.

To my children and grandchildren.

Pastor James LaFavor

***

In dedication to loving memory of my dear mother, who encouraged me to have strong faith.

To my wife, Norlene, and my sons, Trahern, Michael, and Joshua, who inspired me.

Dr. Trahern LaFavor

Contents

Foreword iii

Meet the Authors vi

Dedication viii

Introduction 1

Chapter 1 Identify Relational Problems 3

Chapter 2 What Causes Division in Relationships? 79

Chapter 3 Loving Yourself 115

Chapter 4 Finding Purpose and Meaning 136

Chapter 5 Discovering a Path to Personal Enrichment ... 151

Chapter 6 Developing Habits that Serve You 190

Chapter 7 Finding a Pathway to Spiritual Enrichment ... 214

Chapter 8 Closeness 234

Chapter 9 Build Relationship Bonds 251

Chapter 10 Now What? 268

x

Introduction

Pastor James

Family closeness is an innate universal need. Throughout history, many have gleaned from the safety, support, and sense of identity offered from the foundation of the family. To preserve the family unit, we must search for tools to inspire individuals and families to discover pathways to strengthen family relational bonds. Why are family bonds important?

According to the National Institute of Health (NIH), family relationships provide resources that can help an individual cope with stress, engage in healthier behaviors, and enhance self-esteem, leading to higher well-being.

This book is an easy-to-read guide to avenues and pathways to close the gap in our relationships. I sincerely believe that through prayer and humility, we can heal much of the disconnect that arises in family systems.

Rebuilding & Repairing Relationships (The three R's) is a book about restoring and repairing relationships that have been ruptured or damaged. This process of fixing relational brokenness can be a daunting task. We hope that this book will provide some insight into how to repair your relationships.

Dr. Trahern (Tron)

Life is not easy. We all face insurmountable challenges. But the key is overcoming those difficulties. Repairing relationships is about being an overcomer. No matter what relational challenge you face, you can continue to persevere.

According to *Positive Psychology,* perseverance refers to our ability to pursue a goal or passion over time and stick with it even if we encounter obstacles or setbacks. What is your initial response to a relational challenge? Do you fret or stress? Do you lose hope? Perhaps you engage in self-defeating habits.

Our hope is that this handbook will provide a guide to solving some of the relationship difficulties you face. Many times, it requires going back to the drawing board and creating an action plan despite the obstacles you face.

The adversities of life test our foundation. Although we don't have answers to some of life's difficulties, we can press on. May the insights in *Rebuilding & Repairing Relationships* (The three R's) inspire you to work through the relational challenges you've faced.

Chapter 1

Identify Relational Problems

"Bearing with one another and, if one has a complaint against another, forgiving each other; as the Lord has forgiven you, so you also must forgive. And above all these put on love, which binds everything together in perfect harmony."

Colossians 3:13-14 ESV

"We repeat what we don't repair."

– John Gottman

Pastor James

For over forty years, I have pastored in South Florida. This has been a privilege and an opportunity. It has been my passion to help individuals and families find a pathway to hope. It has been an educational and rewarding experience to provide relief to people. I have witnessed people during the emotional highs and lows of their lives. Over the years, many have come to my office seeking help for children and families experiencing behavioral challenges. I have also counseled husbands and wives seeking relational advice. I have always been grateful for the opportunity to reach out and provide guidance and help to those drifting apart in their relationships.

Bridging the gap of relational brokenness is a journey. Because there are unexpected twists and turns in families, I begin the process by having the clients write down what they feel is causing the conflict in their relationship. Then, I show them each other's perspective. This step requires a toolbox of skills, such as knowledge, training, empathy, compassion, and listening skills. As a counselor, I not only listen to words expressed during sessions, but I also listen to feelings. I believe listening attentively gives insights into their problems from a different perspective. For instance, we all know physical wounds require specific treatment for proper healing. But how does one heal from a wounded heart, injured emotions, or feelings of exhaustion? This book sheds light on the healing process.

The goal of repairing relationships is to provide practical ways to help disrupt the patterns of thinking and behaving that lead to relational problems.

At the beginning of this chapter, Colossians chapter 3 was quoted. I believe this scripture verse sheds light on behaviors and attitudes necessary to bridge the gap of family disunity. It also gives practical spiritual intervention. I view effective intervention as a prescription for problems. But the treatment must be applied. The best medicine does not do any good unless applied. Likewise, effective spiritual intervention is necessary to strengthen impaired relationships and unite family members.

In unpacking Paul's advice in Colossians 3, he advises us to refrain from holding anger against each other. He offers insights on demonstrating care and concern for one another. Perhaps understanding, care, and concern are missing in troubled family relationships. I believe increasing understanding, care, and concern can shift the focus from imperfections or shortcomings to empathy for others. Although challenging, we must strive to be empathetic and understanding towards each other. We need to search for spiritual principles to rectify emotional and character defects to become unstuck in our personal relations.

My vocation as a pastor and a counselor continues to bring me inexpressible joy and personal satisfaction. Preaching and counseling are my true calling. As a child in elementary school, I had a desire to help others. I felt good about doing things for others. I used to search for ways to inspire my classmates. As a youngster, I loved observing vehicles. I was fascinated by the make and model of any automobile. I used to draw a good depiction of any make or model of any automobile. My friends got a great deal of satisfaction from my sketches of cars. In return, I got a good feeling from creating something that made my peers happy. I discovered helping people feel good caused me to feel better inside. My passion for helping others continued to grow. For instance, I had abilities in math and reading. I used to assist other students struggling with their lessons. This task also gave me a sense of joy. Giving a helping hand was a rewarding experience.

Growing up, I witnessed many children and families who were afflicted by painful maladies. I hoped to lessen the pain or do something to make the world a better place when I got older.

A Little History

I grew up in a small rural town in Louisville, Georgia. Reflecting on those days, there seemed to be very little to feel good about. Everyone was poor. There was widespread scarcity and lack. Many families experienced brokenness, pain, and disconnections. Even though we had little in terms of possessions, we had each other. Both my parents experienced struggles. My father began working at twelve years old. The unexpected death of my grandfather required him to step into manhood early on.

My mother's parents passed away when she was about five years old. This loss caused anxiety and depression. Although she experienced challenges in life, she found relief in helping the less fortunate around her. I learned much of my compassion, care, and concern for helping others from my mother. From my youth, my mother always told me that I was born to be a minister of the gospel. Such predictions continue to have a great impression on me. I have always had a soft place in my heart for all people. I always desired to give authentic love. With this foundation, I began to aspire to become a relationship builder.

As I began my journey, I started to become curious. Questions such as how some individuals and families were able to control their actions and behaviors better than others puzzled me. Even though family backgrounds and systems were similar, some families got along well, while others were constantly at odds. As I grew older, I began to seek methods to bring families closer. I started with my own family of origin. I often wondered if I could ever establish genuine bonds of peace, harmony, and commitment in my personal relationships. I learned doing good pays dividends. I found doing good to others is truly a pathway to a helping vocation.

My first experience in the helping ministry started in a small church called the Spiritual Church of God and Christ. The encouragement and push of the pastor's wife inspired me to pursue the pathway to ministry. The pastor and his wife recognized my honesty and that I wanted to be a difference-maker.

In my mind, education was essential in ministry. I expanded my knowledge and self-development by studying sociology, psychology, and religion.

First, I needed to learn about human emotions, which I knew nothing about. This included emotional control, understanding one's personality, and relational skills. This step was important because my own cherished relationships needed improving. When my awareness of emotional insight increased, my relationships became enriched and developed. This sparked my passion. The doors of opportunity opened for me to begin my ministry. I had what the Bible calls a spiritual awakening. I desired to preach and help others. Studying the scriptures, I found solutions to fix and mend broken relationships. Those estranged in disconnected families could be brought closer together. How does this work?

As a pastor over the years, I have worked with individuals addicted to drugs, single parents, and broken family units. My passion for pastoring and counseling aided me in developing programs to meet the needs of the members. Having a heart for others, I was ready to work on this goal.

Case example 1

I recall a case in my ministry referred by my wife. One day, she called from her job, saying, "I have someone that I would like you to talk to."

I will refer to this man as Joe. I could sense in Joe's voice that he was struggling with excessive amounts of anxiety and guilt. Joe was forty years old. His poor decision-making undermined all his relations. I begin the conversation by showing empathy. I assured him I understood what he was going through and that we wanted to help.

On Sunday, my wife invited Joe to church. When I met Joe, I felt compassion for him. He seemed to be a humble soul. As we talked, he informed me that he used to teach Sunday School for a few years. By the expression on his face, I saw he felt good about things in his life. I saw this as a window of opportunity. I offered Joe some spiritual interventions to help with his addiction. Over time, through listening without judgment, he was able to put some distance between himself and his addictions. Through counseling and spiritual guidance, he could move back home with his family and begin repairing his relationships.

Case example 2

I would like to consider another case I had the privilege to work on as a chaplain and therapist at a mental health hospital in South Florida. During my eighteen and a half years, I worked with patients suffering from an array of severe mental disorders. One case that stands out is a patient suffering from a deep religious fixation. This individual was experiencing an intense belief. In his delusion, he purported he was Christ. As the chaplain and mental health therapist, I supported the treatment team. I was called upon to offer support and care. I provided a biblical plan to guide him back to scriptural reality.

Firstly, I did not challenge his delusional belief. I took him on my rounds. He was my assistant. He would always carry my Bible without hesitation. This task gave him a sense of pride. As we walked onto units, he would assist in helping other delusional patients. As I talked with patients, he offered support. During services, he would do opening prayers. He would also read positive scriptures that boosted his feelings. Secondly, he began applying the selected scriptures reading to his life. He slowly began to connect valid scripture.

From month to month, he started to improve in his faulty thinking. In about three months of this spiritual treatment, he changed. Instead of declining medicine, he willingly took his prescribed medications and participated in other enrichment programs. In a few more months, he was discharged from the hospital and was able to go on with his life.

The necessity for self-forgiveness: The holistic approach to ministry is my way or model of helping ministry.

How does one heal from relational feelings of brokenness? We all know physical wounds require specific treatment for proper healing. But how does one heal from a wounded heart, injured emotions, or feelings of exhaustion?

The goal of repairing relationships is to provide practical ways to help disrupt the patterns of thinking and behaving that lead to relational problems.

The abovementioned verse in Colossians chapter 3 provides a treatment for improving relationships. Firstly, we learned to bear with the behaviors and attitudes causing family disunity. It points out spiritual interventions we need to employ in our lives so we chart a pathway toward closing the gap in impaired relations.

Secondly, Paul gives practical guidance for bringing family members together. We are advised to refrain from holding anger against each other but persist in demonstrating care and concern for each other.

Lastly, he encourages us to strive to be empathetic and understanding toward each other. We need to search for spiritual principles to rectify emotional and character defects that are stuck in our personal relations. Gottman's quote says, "We repeat what we don't repair." I interpret this to mean we need to stop doing the same thing, hoping for different outcomes. Life is about seeing where we are going wrong and making a change.

Dr. Trahern (Tron)

For more than sixteen years, I have had the privilege of working with youth and families presenting with severe emotional and behavioral problems. My career began as an in-home therapist in Fort Lauderdale, Florida.

There was one case I will never forget. I received a call from a frantic mother. In tears, she expressed that her son, who was low functioning, was influenced by a group of negative peers to commit a crime. My heart raced as I provided her with support to navigate that trying time in her life.

I have sat at many dining room tables and on sofas discussing problems parents face rearing their children, such as verbal aggression, physical aggression, poor academics, negative peer associations, ineffective parenting, and emotional and behavioral difficulties.

I am moved to compassion when I witness firsthand the struggles parents encounter daily. Reflecting on my work, it's difficult to hear people say, "These youth must be taught a lesson through severe consequences." I see their lives through a different lens. As a result, I am inclined to show mercy. The way you look at the world shifts when you go behind the scenes. In graduate studies, I learned all behavior makes sense in context. This means you need the full context or picture to understand isolated behavior. For instance, a single mother does not have support and struggles to make ends meet. The low monitoring may cause her child to engage with negative peers while she is working.

How about the grandparents who adopted their grandchildren to avoid them being removed and sent to foster care or the older sibling forced to step into the shoes of parenthood at such a young age? All these experiences have made me empathetic as I walk into the homes of struggling families. It is rewarding to help a parent, grandparent, or caregiver overcome challenges. Repairing families is about providing tools, skills, insight, wisdom, and knowledge to overcome difficulties. It has been twenty years since I was released from the National Football League (NFL). When I left, the coach said, "Tron, we have to let you go, but you will be okay."

Being okay meant going back home to lift others up as I had been lifted. Not only can I share a dream, but I can inspire hope that it is possible to reach your goals. When I walked into the homes of children who had been abused and neglected, my boss said, "Tell the children you used to play in the NFL."

One puzzled youth asked,

"Why did you leave the NFL to be a counselor? You would have made more money if you had stayed there."

I would smile and say, "I am happy to be here, helping you."

My journey from the inner city of Fort Lauderdale to the NFL has taught me many life lessons. These life lessons inform my counseling and ministry work; I firmly believe you can reach your God-given potential in life. From my lived experience and training, I can provide a blueprint and tools for navigating the difficulties and uncertainties of life.

Rebuilding & Repairing Relationships aims to provide strategies to enhance human relationships and offer practical tools for overcoming life's challenges. Although these maladies strain us and our relationships, we can be overcomers.

Identify Relational Problems

Dr. Gottman's quote says, "We repeat what we don't repair." I interpret this to mean we need to stop doing the same thing, hoping for different outcomes. Life is about seeing where we are going wrong and making a change.

Relational Challenges

Pastor James LaFavor,

As a pastor, I know what it is like to experience relational challenges. I define relational challenges as a negative experience that impacts one's life. When I came to Florida over sixty years ago, I had $20 in my pocket and did not know how to make ends meet. But by connecting to a Bible teaching church and serving as a mentor, I succeeded. I worked through relational challenges in marriage and raised five children. My responsibilities consisted of family life, pastoring a church, and work life. I have learned how to navigate life's challenges. When my wife died at the age of seventy-three, I had to use the tools I will share in this book to make it through.

Personal Challenges

Pastor James

When I think of personal challenges, I think about faith, determination, persistence, and perseverance in the face of hardships. These are action principles for confronting relational challenges.

Personal challenges are an essential part of life. All individuals face them. What are personal challenges? Personal challenges are bumps and problems on the horizon of life that get in the way of success. There are some challenges that are common to all people, whether you are rich or poor. Issues of anxiety, depression, physical or social difficulties, and low self-esteem. These challenges, among others, are prevalent among all people. The key is learning how to navigate building a healthy, mature life. Now, I would like to look back at some of the personal challenges I had to deal with in my quest to build a good life. I truly hope that as I share my personal challenges, you will be encouraged to confront your challenges.

Relational Challenges

Dr. Trahern (Tron)

I define relational challenges as conflicts that undermine relationships. The key to handling relational challenges is learning to cope. These challenges come in many forms. In my mid-twenties, I faced a career challenge. After being released from the NFL, I had to rebuild and start over again. Perhaps you are facing hardships. Are you rebuilding or repairing your life? Many are rebuilding after the loss of a loved one; others are rebuilding after the loss of a job, and many are rebuilding after terminal illness. Countless are working to hold families together. Whatever difficulty you are facing, keep the faith and never stop hoping.

> "Hope is not pretending that troubles don't exist. It is the trust that they will not last forever, that hurts will be healed and difficulties overcome. It is faith that a source of strength and renewal lies within to lead us through the dark into the sunshine."
>
> — Liz Chase

Personal Challenges

Dr. Trahern (Tron)

Personal challenge, in its simplest form, is something that is hard to do or overcome. It is so personally challenging that it interferes with one's life, making it difficult to achieve goals. It's like a roadblock that gets in the way of one's destiny.

As an adolescent, when times were rough, my father said, "Son, when life is tough, grab the bull by the horns."

At the time, I did not grasp the full meaning of what my dad was saying, but later I discovered what it meant. He was telling me to hold on and keep going no matter how tough it gets.

One day, I picked up the book *Tough Times Never Last, But Tough People Do*. I learned a valuable lesson from the book. When life is tough, we must become tougher. My father stressed that life is like a bull ride. There are ups, downs, twists, and turns. But a good rider gets back on even when he is thrown off the bull. Perhaps you have been knocked down. Life is about dusting yourself off and getting back on the ride. Here are some action steps that are helpful in overcoming challenges.

First, we must identify the challenge. This means developing a clear picture of the problem and its influence on our lives. When I was in graduate school studying the models of family therapy, I learned a technique from narrative therapy called externalizing the problem. This meant I am not the problem; the problem is the problem, and I must act on it.

Second, when the problem is identified, a good formula for dealing with it must be developed. One of my clients used to go out in nature and employ prayer and study of the scripture to deal with his problem.

Third, find a competent counselor to help you deal with the challenges you face.

Fourth, develop a positive attitude of gratitude. Practice gratitude daily and count your blessings. Instead of looking at what we don't have, let's look at what we do have.

Fifth, let go of the past and things you can't control. We can't drive a vehicle looking in the rearview mirror. If we do, we will crash. Stop looking at past mistakes and failures. Let us continue to move towards a brighter future.

Sixth, think big, don't have small thinking, believe in your possibilities. You can be who you were born to be. Discover the things that will give purpose and meaning to your life. Perhaps you need to take some action steps, such as returning to school, getting a certification, or starting a hobby or business. Whatever it is, do it. Maybe developing yourself spiritually or building your relationships.

About Dealing with Personal Challenges

Pastor James

Understanding and challenging our true personal feelings is difficult. It requires insight and great effort. The analysis of the expressions of feelings takes courage.

We need a deep commitment on how to understand our emotions more fully. Understanding and recognizing how we feel is vital to our wellness. Knowing how we feel and why helps us to understand ourselves and build relationships. Understanding how we feel also helps us regulate and control our feelings, which leads to a more fulfilling life. How did my personal feelings impact my life growing up? A deep level of emotional understanding in my adolescence was an overbearing process. The issue of tension and the stress of low self-esteem made me weary. Dealing with the feelings that life brought me was my greatest challenge. But in the midst of these feelings, there was a pathway. Thanks be to God; through study and hard work, we can raise our emotional intelligence. Writing this chapter has inspired and informed my interest tremendously in the importance of emotional understanding.

I hope that reading this information will be of some encouragement to you. Rasing self-assurance is difficult but not impossible. It can be a rewarding challenge. It is just another hill to climb toward the enhancement of a richer life. Have courage; don't be afraid to go against your feelings of inadequacy.

Make it a habit every day. We can embrace our challenges and the subsequent opportunities for growth and learning experiences. Let us make them a personal contest for overcoming our limitations.

To fix your relationship with yourself and others, you must be determined to succeed. You must resolve that you will pay the price, no matter the time or effort it will take to reach your desired outcome. Believe that you can power your way into your purpose. With faith and surrender to the Highest Power, we can press our way on through the challenges of life. Sometimes, baby steps are required. But just persist. When we are born into this world, the battle for life has started. One of the greatest battles that we will ever fight is the battle with our emotions.

As an adolescent, one of my significant challenges was understanding how to deal with my feelings. I had no idea what processing my emotions meant. The big challenge was to understand that it was okay to feel and express one's feelings, whether we feel joy, happiness, or sadness, which greatly impacts how we experience life. We need to know that no matter how we feel or what we are going through, we can master our feelings. Understanding my feelings and other people's feelings was a struggle for me. I was spending too much time in my feelings. Feelings are much more complex than most people realize. Emotions can be very difficult to evaluate. I believe a lack of emotional intelligence is a foundation for unfavorable regard for oneself. The key is to become aware of self-acceptance and knowledge of one's personal strengths. The same scrutiny applies to the repair of all wounded relationships. We must identify the problem and seek a competent counselor. The problem of low self-esteem has a lot to do with the environment that we were raised in.

When I was a youngster, I knew a kid who was raised by his grandmother. She was a gracious soul. But she was somewhat old-fashioned. The grandson had to wear a cap and short pants everywhere he went. Other children would steal his cap and hide it. His grandmother would make him go and find it. This act was funny to the children. This kid developed a sense of insecurity from the careless pranks of his peers. Even in adulthood, he would always look at people with apprehension.

Good religion and spirituality can help us master our emotions. But we must keep on seeking until we find the fantastic key that unlocks the door. What are some of the barriers to realizing your best life? The desire to fit in presented problems for me. As a youth, I always wanted to fit in and feel accepted by peers who dressed better and had more than me. Growing up, I always had the need to belong. Looking back now, I know that these feelings of rejection were not always valid, but they were there. At times, it was my overly sensitive feelings that caused me to feel strong emotions. Many times, I felt overwhelmed and isolated. I became very good at masking my feelings. So, I had to learn and grow. You have to dig your heels in and find solutions to elevate your feelings. I found some answers to my problems in the wisdom of the scripture. According to the Bible, we can have the mind of Christ. Take, for instance, Philippians 2:5. Based on this scripture, we, as believers, can share in the wisdom and supernatural power of Christ's intelligence. With this spiritual insight, our perspective of ourselves and the world can change in a true way. Another Bible verse states that we are all God's children, created in His image. Just apply faith in the ultimate power. So, the first thing that I needed to do was to find out what was the cause of my low self-esteem, and poverty had been one of my roadblocks as a youth.

Growing up in strict poverty presented a great challenge for me. I learned that children growing up in poverty experience long-lasting negative effects. Poverty affects children physically, emotionally, mentally, and socially. These deficiencies can have adverse consequences in adulthood. Experiencing hunger, malnutrition, and emotional and social problems can make you feel unaccepted and left out.

Not having one's basic needs met opens the door to a downward spiral, leading to low self-esteem. One year in middle school, my school wardrobe consisted of one pair of Wrangler jeans, one red flannel shirt, and one pair of cheap loafers. This wardrobe had to last the entire school year. Twice per week, I had to wash this outfit by hand. Sometimes, my jeans would still be damp in the morning. I would have to put them on to wear to school. It was tough getting out of bed to attend school at times. However, I had to muster up the strength to keep going. Where did I get the motivation to keep going in this season of lack? There is something deep within all of us that can keep us going in the face of tests, but we must find it.

Staying in school was a test for many males of my generation. It was tough to keep going when you knew that you could drop out of school and earn five or six dollars a day. Sometimes, people quit because they felt responsible for financially assisting their families. Young boys had a passion for buying their first automobile. They just wanted to have a few decent clothes, which they never had before. I was driven by the same desire for a while. I eventually dropped out of school in the eighth grade for only one year. It did not take me very long to realize that coming into the possession of a few cheap material things was worth nothing in comparison to a high school education. It was the positive influence of a few people that inspired me to rise up and press on.

I have never forgotten what our high school principal wrote in our graduation yearbook. He wrote, "You are now ready to go out into a world torn by strife and racism. So, you must be ready to make your mark in the world." From this message, I knew that it would not be easy. It was time to confront the world. The scripture admonishes us always to be guided by integrity. Then we won't go wrong. Honesty is a powerful driving force.

We must desire to be led by integrity. No matter what others around me were doing, I saw the value of trying to choose the right thing; taking a stand was not easy. The saying is true that hardship is a pathway to peace. My mother and father always told us to do the right thing. My dad would often add to the admonition that it is not so hard to do the right thing if you choose to do so. I found these principles to be a true way of transcending difficult circumstances. Transcending difficult challenges can be very hard, and change can be trying. But, when we diligently seek the help of the Highest Power, the universe gets behind us. The human mind wants to move forward, but we must do our part.

About Dealing with Personal Challenges

Dr. Trahern (Tron)

In 2007, I entered the field of marriage and family therapy to help families create lasting and meaningful changes in their lives. What gives meaning to my work is I have experienced my own personal challenges in life. I know the feeling of losing a dream job and having to start all over again on a new dream. I experienced the pain of watching my mother in her final hours. During that heartbreaking time, I found a place of peace. It was the faith I learned at her knee that got me through. Perhaps you have some difficulties to work through. Maybe you feel like you are in the middle of the ocean. It seems hopeless, but do not panic; help is on the way.

As a Christian therapist, I have discovered sound faith and scientific treatment are a remedy for any problem. If your life is veering off track, you can take control of the wheel and drive into purposeful living. My hope is that reading *Rebuilding & Repairing Relationships* will help guide you along the path of meaningful relationships.

Some believe it is a stigma to seek help, but there are times in life when we need the support of a professional to help us navigate life's challenges.

Since relationships come in all shapes and sizes, I will use scenarios I have witnessed to repair relational problems. To maintain confidentiality, pseudonyms are used in this book.

Examples of Relational Problems

Scenario 1

Nancy and Mike are married and have four children. Nancy decided to sacrifice a career as a businesswoman to be a stay-at-home mother. Over time, she began to experience marital problems. She became critical of her husband, who worked many hours in construction. Nancy started to disempower Mike and focus on his faults. She frequently pointed out all his weak points, such as sleeping too long and not communicating.

Scenario 2

Tiffany (twenty-two years old) and Felicity (twenty-one years old) are siblings who grew up in Cleveland, Ohio. They always enjoyed a close bond. But over time, their relationship was strained. It all started when Tiffany felt that Felicity was getting more attention from their parents. Felicity constantly excelled in academics and athletics. It appeared she was the golden child of the family. Tiffany felt left out and started to believe she was not good enough. Even though her parents attended all her recitals, it was not enough for her. Her thought pattern was fixed on Felicity as the favored child. Tiffany kept these emotions hidden and bottled up for a year. No one really knew how she felt. However, the signs begin to show because she disconnected from her family of origin when she became an adult. Tiffany began to isolate herself from her family and did not return phone calls or attend family events.

Identify Relational Problems

One day at work, Tiffany exploded emotionally on a coworker who was getting all the recognition. To avoid losing her job, it was strongly recommended that she seek professional help.

Scenario 3

George is seventeen years old. He grew up in the suburbs. He is the youngest of the three. The people in George's community saw him as a troubled youth. Everywhere he went, he was targeted. George always felt inferior because of his short and chubby stature. As an adolescent, he was frequently suspended from school. He spent more days out of school than in school. Due to multiple suspensions, he began to lose hope. He also had an encounter with the police because he threw a rock and broke his neighbor's window. George's parents, Casey and Charlie, tried everything they could to help George, but nothing worked. He went to many counselors, but there was no change.

Scenario 4

Myles is a retired schoolteacher. After thirty years of teaching students in the inner city, he became depressed, and he lacked drive and motivation. His daily routine consists of watching his favorite TV shows and eating fast food. During a recent doctor visit, the physician recommended that Myles become more active. Because he is borderline diabetic, without a drastic lifestyle change, things will get worse. Myles feels overwhelmed and does not know what to do. He has no family support.

The aforementioned case scenarios will be used for the remainder of this book. Each chapter will discuss solutions to solve the problems from the scenarios above. Although the challenges you experience may be different than the ones in our scenarios, we hope you will benefit from the interventions to solve the problems. The goal of repairing relationships is to provide a practical guide for individuals, couples, families, and those in the helping profession.

What causes relational challenges? We will discuss this, and then Dr. LaFavor will define the issue from a clinical perspective.

Dealing with Difficult People

Pastor James

Dealing with difficult people is part of life. Often, we can turn negativity into motivation to press forward. At this time in my life, I was beginning to learn that God loves us, and He will faithfully act as the petition of him who seeks Him.

How can we define difficult people? According to the Bible, a difficult person is someone who lacks empathy and care for others.

Difficult people often imitate the people they grew up around. For example, consider Mary and Sue. They grew up in a large family. They were about one and a half years apart in age. They had the same level of upbringing. They came from a relatively poor family, and they are both older women who cannot get along. They love and need each other. How would I help them? By ministering to these ladies from an integrated approach, I concluded that they were still carrying unresolved anger and hurt feelings from early childhood, which manifested in their inability to get along.

I believe the key question is what drives this negative behavior into adulthood. By thinking about exploring these questions, we gain valuable insights into what drives such negative behavior.

Firstly, we can get along better with negative people. Secondly, we are able to be more empathetic with negative people. Many of these people are people that we love and desire to help. So, what does research show about why some people are compelled by negativity? Studies show that some people are wired to focus on and are more vulnerable to negative information (Verywellmind.com).

Case example

Susan works as a Human Resource Professional. She states that negative people are the most draining people to be around. For the most part, we can avoid negativity, but when we are in the workplace, it can feel impossible to get away from them. They can be tense and stressful to our well-being. As we learn about some of the key reasons that some individuals are so negative, this should move our hearts to have more empathy as we deal with difficult family members. If we are willing to search, we can find good tips for dealing with difficult people. Difficult people are a part of the world. They are in the marketplace. They are part of our family units, jobs, churches, and other social systems.

However, most people are not so difficult to get along with. Negative people will be encountered in all human relationships. What causes some people to be so difficult to deal with? It is said that difficult people are that way usually because they are unhappy about something else; perhaps they grew up in an environment where there was criticism (Embolden Psychology). According to some, if the primary reason is mindsets, that can be caused by many things. As we look at some of the root causes of some people's actions and high levels of negative interactions, it will help us have more empathy for them.

Dealing with negative attitudes, according to Adult.com, may be due to hurt, pain, abuse, and other things that have happened to them in childhood.

Overreactions

Difficult people may be experiencing troubling issues, other negative people, or often stuck in pain or hurt from their childhood. They may be suffering from undiagnosed emotional problems as a result of hurt, pain, and abuse in childhood. Sometimes, people who are masking their pain hurt others. When I was attending elementary school, there was a large poor family in my school who picked on and poked laughter at many of us kids.

Getting through elementary and middle school was a test and a great challenge for me. As a youngster from first through sixth grade, I was confronted with harsh ridicule from several unsympathetic peers. There was one particular family who could be merciless on every occasion. They seemed to thoroughly enjoy painfully teasing us. At a young age, I learned strategies for dealing with difficult people. 1. Don't challenge them. Listen actively. 2. Repeat what they say slowly. 3. Don't react to what is said. 4. Use humor. 5. Pray for them. 6. When possible, limit time spent around them. I have learned that these techniques are still effective when dealing with negative people.

Dealing with Difficult People

Pastor James

People are emotional beings. Therefore, it is important to deal with people with kidskin gloves. People are very sensitive, so it is important to deal with people tactfully. Over the years, I have learned to deal with people using effective strategies. For example, I had a client who became belligerent in session. She was dysregulated because of a misunderstanding. I did not make the situation worse by pouring fuel on the fire. On the other hand, I kept a cool, composed, nonreactive demeanor, and she calmed down. It was like a baby falling to sleep in the arms of a calm parent. Her anger just drifted away.

Dealing with Difficult People

Dr. LaFavor

> "When dealing with people, remember you are not dealing with creatures of logic, but with creatures of emotion, creatures bristling with prejudice, and motivated by pride and vanity."
>
> – Dale Carnegie

The next time you are dealing with a challenging person, remember Dale Carnegie's quote. He suggested we are not dealing with creatures of logic but of strong emotions. What are emotions? Emotions are strong feelings triggered by the events and circumstances of life.

If we're going to be successful in handling difficult people, we must be aware of our own emotional triggers. Instead of becoming emotionally involved in a tug-of-war match with a difficult person, let's increase our awareness of the emotional cycle that triggers conflict. I heard a story of a student who wanted a word of wisdom from a philosopher. The philosopher was not available at the time, but after being pressured to give a word of wisdom, the philosopher said awareness, awareness, awareness. Perhaps the next time we are about to fly off the handle, let's remember the words given to the student. On great sports teams, coaches help players become aware of their opponents. This happens through the study of film and the repetition of plays. It is bound to happen; we will encounter challenging people, but how we choose to respond is critical to achieving success.

Many years ago, I provided in-home therapy to a youth and his family. He became upset with his mother and proceeded to use derogatory statements towards me and her. I applied a nonreactive technique; he calmed down and went to his room. One of the keys to dealing with a difficult person is to stay calm and not let them get in your head.

The next time you encounter a difficult person, take a page from Dr. King's book. While giving a talk, he was slapped in the face. Did he fight back? Did he lose his composure? No, he simply responded using weapons of love. So, how do we effectively deal with difficult people? In dealing with people, there are many variables working together simultaneously. It's like an emotional dance. Many years ago, I took ballroom dancing at the University of Florida. It was my first experience with such an undertaking. At the time, I was a 260-pound defensive lineman. My hope was not to step on the ladies' toes. Therefore, I became mindfully aware of every move.

When comparing ballroom dancing to dealing with difficult people, it is necessary not to step on the toes of a difficult person. This means not getting involved in confrontations that lead to feelings of defeat. As mentioned, we are not dealing with creatures of logic. We are in an emotional dance, and if you don't have the right guide, you will step on someone's toes.

I have met countless parents who felt defeated after a verbal assault from an emotional teenager. I have discovered that children are more likely to win an emotional battle. My advice to parents is to drop the tug-of-war rope. These battles happen in many settings with adults as well. I have encountered overwhelmed employees who allowed a colleague to push their buttons.

I have witnessed couples in an emotional boxing match, struggling to agree over small matters. I have interacted with frustrated grandparents who feel like their grandchildren are being kept hostage because of a disgruntled parent.

How do we employ the right moves to avoid these conflicts? I invite you to open yourself to a new world of possibility. What if you allowed insults to roll off your back, like water on a duck's back? What if you changed your program? I tell my parents in therapy to change their emotional hot buttons. Stop allowing individuals to know your button and puppet your reactions.

When we truly understand the emotions of others and ourselves, we have the potential to be more effective in dealing with difficult people.

Here are some common traits I have observed in my work with challenging people.

1. They struggle to control their emotions.
2. They always have an excuse for their behavior.
3. They are quick to criticize and attack others.
4. They always focus on the negative.
5. They exhibit controlling behaviors.
6. They are jealous of the success of others.
7. They are reactive, not good listeners.

Difficult people can be draining. They make it hard to perform tasks at work, school, religious gatherings, and family relationships. Challenging people are everywhere; they stick out like a sore thumb. It is important to gain insight into dealing with those who rub us the wrong way or get under our skin. It is easy to navigate difficult people in brief interactions.

For instance, if you experience road rage or a disgruntled person at the supermarket. It is easy to avoid that big pothole. But what do we do if these individuals are close acquaintances or relatives? I used to hear the saying walk a mile in someone else's shoes. This means we increase our capacity to understand why a person behaves the way they do.

Through increasing our understanding, we can have more empathy. While it may not change them, it will change you. I have discovered that when our perspective changes, we change. So, the next time you are triggered by a relative, take a deep breath and pause. Ask, can you help me understand?

I have met countless families, couples, and individuals who struggle to deal with difficult people. So here are some strategies I recommend to help your relationship flow like streams of water on a hot summer day.

Always remain calm when dealing with someone who is difficult; never allow them to get under your skin or in your head. Always manage your emotions. Emotional management is critical in dealing with negative people. Identify emotional triggers, and ask yourself, what is it about this person that pushes your buttons? Don't let things build up. Find a good time to share how you feel. When having an important discussion, I recommend a change of setting, such as a park, dinner, or beach. Different settings or places can generate meaningful dialogue. If you get stuck or run into a roadblock, as we sometimes will, seek out a competent counselor. This can be like AAA for a relationship. A good counselor is likened to good roadside assistance, which has the right tools to get us unstuck.

A good family therapist views problems within the broader systemic context. Sometimes, we get stuck in the small things and miss the big picture. For instance, Felicity and Tiffany are experiencing sibling conflict in the case example.

This has been brewing ever since they were adolescents. Rather than focusing on Tiffany's outburst, I became curious about times when they are bonding and connecting. I would listen for stories that sometimes go unnoticed in the narrative of difficulty. Remember, when we look at things differently, the things we look at change. This means we must focus on the strengths of the most challenging person, and things will improve over time.

Family Relational Problems

Pastor James

All families face challenges. In my work as a pastor, the first step when meeting with a family is to identify the family problem. As families sit in the vinyl chairs in my office, I see tears stream down their faces as they express the challenges they face. In many instances, breakdowns in communication have led to signs of frequent arguing, angry outbursts, disagreement, avoidance, and physical conflict. In my role as pastor, I aim to help them create solutions to solve their problems. I believe that there are solutions, but like mining for gold, one must dig deep within to find them.

What are some problems that are experienced by all relations? All relationships must deal with an unhealthy dose of equity, fairness, forgiveness, understanding, and empathy. Equity in relations is characterized by the value that each person has gotten or is getting from the relationship that they are part of. The perception that one carries about how they have been treated growing up in their family of origin. Several variables impact an individual's life depending on the attention one has encountered. Some siblings feel that they have gotten the short end of the stick growing up. Merriam-Webster suggests that some have received unfair or unfavorable treatment. In marriage, one partner may feel that he or she bore the brunt of hardship in the relationship.

1. Write your feelings clearly and concisely on paper and send them to the person you are having problems dealing with.
2. Learn to communicate more effectively by acknowledging the feelings of the other person.
3. Seek out a competent therapist.
4. Practice empathy.
5. Pray for spiritual guidance.

By embracing and practicing these principles, the ways of thinking and acting begin to decline. I always give clients a couple of well-known verses from the Bible. I have found that when these Bible verses are put into practice, they always help tremendously.

Colossians 3:23-24

King James Version

^{23} And whatsoever ye do, do it heartily, as to the Lord, and not unto men.

^{24} Knowing that of the Lord ye shall receive the reward of the inheritance: for ye serve the Lord Christ.

The principles of this text show that when you put forth your best effort every day of life, it helps you to have better thinking.

Family Relational Problems

Dr. Trahern (Tron)

Family relational problems can arise between parents, couples, children, siblings, friends, and other important relationships. Since conflicts are inevitable in familial relations, identifying some causes of relational problems is crucial.

The common relational problems I have witnessed in almost two decades of counseling include families arguing, communication problems, fighting over money, jealousy, unfaithfulness, personality clashes, and verbal and physical aggression. Some clinicians view relational problems as linear, suggesting A caused B, and if I change A, B will automatically change.

This idea seems logical. Just change one person's behavior, and the other person will automatically change. However, there are times when problems are not so easy to fix. It's like a train stuck on the tracks. When relationships get stuck, it seems impossible to break free of cycles of conflict. To manage all the variables simultaneously, I take a relational stance to solving problems.

Let's consider scenario three. Instead of viewing George's behavior from a linear point of view, let's consider a systemic lens, which suggests that the family system is greater than the sum of its parts. This means that instead of blaming George, we will survey the whole family system.

For instance, George's behavioral challenges are due to inferiority feelings from childhood. He has poor school performance and socialization with negative peers. The interplay of these factors has led to severe behavior problems.

According to the Institute of Health, relational problems are clinically significant behavioral patterns that occur between or among individuals and are associated with present distress. When families face persistent distress, it can lead to conflict. I define family distress as a family's inability to manage the daily difficulties of life effectively.

If I were to treat George, I would invite his parents into the session to affirm him. I would then explore his academics and highlight times when he was proficient. Finally, I would help him develop relationships with prosocial, positive peers who are on the road to success.

I believe families come to therapy with worn-out tools or sometimes no tools. My job is to provide them with a toolbox of relational competency skills. When I was a boy, I was fascinated by my neighbor, Mr. Jerry. He had a van full of tools. Whenever we had a problem, my father would send me over to Mr. Jerry for the proper tool. Without fail, he always provided the right tools. He still practices carpentry.

Perhaps we have been using the wrong tool to meet life's challenges. Sadly, I've seen many parents using a hammer to tackle problems that required a screwdriver. Instead of talking to their children rationally, they fly off the handle like a broken axe. Far too many families are approaching problems with worn-out tools. When this happens, it leads to family feuds. Family feuds happen because of different beliefs, perspectives, and worldviews.

Sadly, family feuds can cause people to stay upset for extended periods. I talked to a lady who was so upset with her sister that she refused to attend the funeral service of a loved one who was a matriarch in the family.

While it is normal to get angry, what should you do when anger turns bitter, like sour lemons? When I was younger, I loved taking ten-hour road trips to visit family in Georgia. I used to look out the window at the trees, cattle, and early morning sunrises. I was filled with excitement to see the orange clay hills of Georgia and visit my cousins. We used to play many fun games outside. Recently, I looked in the review mirror of those times. I noticed a unique trait about my uncles and aunts. They used to engage in what I called emotionally charged conversations about religion and politics. It looked like a wrestling match of words. But, at the end of the discussions, there was laughter.

Sadly, most families don't end that way. The other day, someone said, "I am changing my phone number and not giving the new number to my sister." This emotional cut-off shocked me as to how one could choose not to have dealings with a family member because of a feud. It appears the family systems are deteriorating, and there is a need for integrative treatment to treat the whole person's mind, body, and spirit.

Identifying Sibling Challenges

Pastor James

It is essential to recognize the challenges that youth face. Resolving sibling conflicts is one of the huge issues siblings are faced with. Discovering how to improve our relationships is one of the most rewarding things that we can engage in.

Challenges are what make life interesting and meaningful. Sometimes, they are very difficult and painful. But we must try with all our might to deal with them. Family dynamics is a very complex institution. Learning how to love one another should be our greatest endeavor. We will always have the same family of origin. It is never too late to work on the development and enrichment of sibling restoration.

Here are some challenges families must deal with. One is the challenge of feelings management. Challenges of social aptitude. Challenges of how to support each sibling equally. Children need continued growth and wisdom. John Woodman said that family love is the most important thing in the world. No one should get left behind. We must continue to invest in ways of empowering and creating closeness, and our family of origin is our greatest investment.

Two Sisters with Conflicting Personalities

These sisters always clash every time they get together. They grew up in a large, Christian, low-income family. I will call them by the names Leslie and Roslyn. Leslie is the older of the two sisters. Leslie is very independent. She is hard-working and self-supporting. Leslie lives alone and has never married. Roslyn, on the other hand, is a widow. She demonstrates far fewer work skills and financial management abilities than Leslie.

Their inability to get along together seems to arise because both are very sensitive and highly opinionated. They talk to each other daily on the phone, but before they end their calls, they always end up angry and argue in conclusion. Sibling rivalry begins way back in childhood. Feelings and actions of jealousy and competition get carried over into adulthood. In the case of Leslie and Rosalyn, they still find themselves quarreling and attacking each other, even in old age.

In our second counseling session, we began to look for an understanding of what may be driving their negative perception of each other. After careful listening to some of the negative qualities of their behavior, apparently, they have carried a jealous, competitive spirit from childhood into adulthood. This spirit has led them to become more and more compulsive in their ability to have reciprocal dialogue. Because of their inability to listen to each other, their conversations always escalate into resentful attacks. So, what are some workable interventions for such self-defeating behaviors?

Some tips for creating closeness in family relations:
1. Start with good, open communication. Try to talk with understanding and care. Listen with compassion and empathy for the other person's thoughts and emotions with care. Avoid responding with criticism of the other person.
2. Be willing to listen to the feelings of each speaker. When we listen to the feelings of others, it helps them feel respected and understood.
3. Avoid being critical of what another person is saying.
4. Work hard to show unconditional love to all family members.
5. Help each member to feel worthy and appreciated.
6. Speak to each other with kindness and respect. Look to the scriptures. The Bible says treat others as you want to be treated. Luke 6:31 And as ye would that men should do to you, do ye also to them likewise. Also, practice treating one another with kindness Ephesians 4:32 And be ye kind one to another, tenderhearted, forgiving one another, even as God for Christ's sake hath forgiven you. So, we can all play a role in creating harmony.

In my work as a pastor, I discovered that siblings often struggle to find their identity within a family system. I have firsthand experience with this. I grew up as the oldest of ten children. My parents did the best they could. My mother and father had third-grade educations. This happened because my father left school when he was twelve years old because his father died. As I reflect on his experience, I can only imagine the pain he felt. It was not easy to have to work in the fields all day long sharecropping. He did this to take care of his mother and sister. This responsibility, as mentioned, led to his withdrawal from school. He had to teach himself how to read.

Furthermore, my mother never knew her parents. She was an orphan. Many days, I watched her shed tears. Some were tears of joy, while others were tears of sorrow. She used to wash clothes, and as she washed, she would burst into singing and crying. These passionate spiritual songs used to grab my attention. With all the difficulties she faced, she maintained joy. Years later, I began to examine their plight. Evidently, their faith in God helped them make it through the tough times. As the saying goes, "Tough times never last, but tough people do." They had a strong belief in God. Today, I am reaping the fruits of their faith. My parents found their identity. Now, I am helping others find theirs. Although a challenge at times, it is possible. When counseling families, I look for the person hidden beneath what appears to be brokenness. I seek to help individuals get connected to their Creator.

Identifying Sibling Challenges

Dr. Trahern (Tron)

Sibling rivalry happens in sibling relationships. This is an occurrence that most parents must contend with when raising children. Sibling rivalry can be defined as feelings of jealousy and competition that show up in sibling relationships. Perhaps you have encountered this intense conflict between siblings. This happens in biological siblings, stepsiblings, and adoptive siblings.

Many factors contribute to sibling rivalry, such as personality traits, feelings, and temperament. These factors create a power struggle between siblings. This competition for attention is something parents must contend with in the formative years of youth development.

As children get older, they tend to grow out of these feelings as they mature. But sometimes, one gets stuck and needs assistance sorting out unresolved feelings. Parents must be mindful of the tactics employed in dealing with children in the sibling rivalry combat zone. If not, they can contribute to these feelings. It's like pouring gasoline on a fire. For instance, in the above scenario, Felicity and Tiffany grew up in a home with both parents. Early in the sibling relationship, jealousy and competition showed up.

How do feelings of jealousy happen in close sibling relationships? I believe parents and relatives play a role in sibling rivalry. Because one child is praised over another, such feelings are triggered that contribute to this behavior.

One of the common feelings that are triggered is a sense of insecurity. Insecurities are feelings of inadequacy, lack of confidence or not being good enough (www.webmd.com). I have discovered when siblings wrestle with unresolved insecurities and low confidence, it spills over into adulthood.

> "When you let go of your bitterness, inadequacy, & incompleteness, the more you tap into your true creative genius. Unchain your inner voice!"
>
> — Assegid Habtewold

I recently talked to a mother who brought a new child home, but the older sibling was upset because he had to share his mother with his brother. These feelings show up early in the sibling relationship and require insight and awareness to unpack this emotional baggage.

How to treat sibling rivalry

In therapy, I listen to stories that contribute to sibling rivalry. As a practitioner, I am always curious to explore when a problem appears in a person's life or narrative. In narrative therapy, there is a technique called externalizing problems. This helps the client see the problems they face from a different perspective. This technique helps the client get to the root of their problem. Like a gardener whose responsibility is cultivating healthy plants, I facilitate change by cultivating healthy relationships with those who were once chained by jealousy, fear, resentment, and insecurity.

In our illustration, Felicity was perceived as the golden child because of parental praise lavished on her. Tiffany felt left out. This happened because the parents, consciously or unconsciously, praised her sister and left her out. Felicity was always praised for her academic efforts, but Tiffany felt she did not receive a fair share of praise. One of the mishaps is that parents fail to clearly see each child's potential, skills, abilities, or talents.

For instance, if a parent is a dancer, and a child engages in dance like their parent, the parent may be more inclined to develop an emotional bond with that child. But another child of theirs who engages in arts and sciences may feel disconnected if that same parent doesn't show interest in their skill. Parents should engage all children equally, even if it's an area that is unnatural to them.

The best cure for sibling rivalry is for parents to reduce or refuse to compare their children. Planning family activities together is a way to reduce sibling rivalry.

Here are six strategies to reduce sibling rivalry.

1. Parents should treat children fairly.
2. Encourage teamwork.
3. Refuse to uphold one child while leaving the other child out.
4. Praise all children equally.
5. Teach problem-solving skills.
6. Listen to children's feelings.

Dating Challenges

Pastor James

Dating is that process where two people start a relationship to determine if suitability and likability for each other is there. These balanced actions are necessary to understand if your values are similar enough. The key to overcoming dating challenges is to start right. The challenges in getting to know another person is not easy. Honesty is the pathway to the doorway for the entrance to effective relationship building. The house will crumble if there are no fundamental principles at the bottom. Fundamental principles are those principles that have endured the test of time.

Tony grew up in a family where the mother was very emotional, demanding, and controlling. She dominated every aspect of the affairs of the home. She would become very upset if her husband purchased as much as a shirt without her approval. But she would spend money on expensive items without her husband's knowledge. There were two children in the family, a son and a daughter. The daughter was disabled and never married. On the other hand, the son was attracted to the kind of controlling women with the same personality traits as his mother. His marriages would always end up in divorce. He continued to be attracted to the same kind of relationships. It is very important to have knowledge of the challenges that one will encounter in order to build a solid relationship. Lasting unions must be weighed and balanced through the dating process. Getting to know one another is to understand what makes them tick.

Challenges are something that both partners will encounter. The secret is you must know what you want. The qualities listed below are the kind of building blocks that have been tested for establishing the cohesive bond. Take notice of some elements that are essential to the formulation of all mutual and satisfying connections. Look for chemistry between yourself and your partner.

If there is a lack of chemistry, misplaced values, and unwillingness to work on the relationship, it will cause pressure. But knowing what you want can help you avoid mental pressures, harassment, and jealousy. These are aspects that must not be glossed over when considering a mate.

What can make dating easy? Where should you start?

The chemistry connection in a relationship is the foundational pillar of an emotional connection between the two partners. A deep understanding of trust and intimacy is also vital. Emotional partnership is the ability to connect on a deep level of interconnection. Good chemistry helps couples align their values. When your values agree, individuals can understand what they are willing to give toward the development of a reciprocal relationship. These qualities help to empower the partners to deal with pressure and stress in a more effective way. So, transcending the challenges of healthy bonding in a relationship will require spending time together and doing things together.

Getting to know each other fully will require insights into who we are and what we want.

How do you know when you have a good foundation for establishing a fruitful relation? Leave no stones unturned when searching for common attributes for establishing a lasting relationship.

Finding commonalities is a challenge that many dating couples face. In premarital counseling, I seek to find core values to secure a firm relational foundation. This is not easy because baggage from unresolved relationships can block such a connection. The first thing I want to find out about dating couples is whether they have a love for God. Then, I assess their commitment to each other. In over forty years in the helping profession, I have discovered that couples with a God-centered relationship do much better than those without. Therefore, my job as a pastor is to ensure that couples get off to a good start. The best way to do this is to ensure that God is at the center of all their relationships. Also, I encourage young couples to find a place to serve God and others.

Dating Challenges

Dr. Trahern (Tron)

One of the most common challenges I have observed in individuals dating is finding someone with similar values willing to commit to a monogamous relationship. In this section, I will provide insights to help individuals who desire a committed relationship.

Have you ever been in a relationship, wanting more while the other person wanted less? Perhaps you wanted more time, while the other partner wanted time apart. Or maybe you were at a crossroads, longing to know which direction the relationship is going. You desired more, while your partner expressed things were fine just the way they were.

Longing to hear, "Let's take the next step," you were perplexed by the opposite words: "I just want to be friends."

After years of investing time and energy, these six words have caused many to lose hope of a meaningful relational future. It is not easy to look at the remnants of broken promises. Like the hallways of an empty room, broken promises echo in the ears of hurting hearts. I have sat with many couples who could not make the mental and emotional adjustment of commitment.

Instead of diving into the ocean of true and lasting love, they stood on the shores of fear and despondency. And the hope of a meaningful relationship slipped through their fingers like sand on the shores.

Unanswered questions can leave one spent and confused during the dating process. The wisest man to ever live illustrated empty promises as clouds without rain. Many have looked for showers of joy, bliss, and fulfillment to rain upon their relationship, only to be left with flashes of lightning and thunder and feelings of despair.

According to Wikipedia, dating is a stage of romantic relationships in which two individuals engage in an activity together, most often with the intention of evaluating each other's suitability as partners in a future intimate relationship.

While stability is the goal of dating, many individuals experience mistrust because relationships that start off promising end bitterly. My hope is to share ways to help individuals avoid the pitfall of broken promises. If you desire a committed relationship, here are some tips from my clinical work to safeguard and guide your decisions regarding dating.

1. Before you begin your next relationship, write down your relational goals.
2. List the details in personality, character traits, and values that are necessary for your mate.
3. Review your list before and after the date when meeting a potential candidate. It compares to HR reviewing a resume for a job interview. This avoids time wasters.
4. Ask the potential candidate what their relational goal is.
5. Be transparent about your emotional needs. Find out what they believe is necessary to make a relationship work.

Marital Challenges

Pastor James

"If I get married, I want to be very married."

— Audrey Hepburn

It pays to get marriage right. According to research, communication, trust, money, intimacy, differences in personality, and in-laws are the biggest problems in marriage (www.Strawpoll.com).

The key challenge to a good marriage is acquiring the wisdom to live a God-centered life. This means making God your priority in your marriage. Marriage is defined as the interpersonal union that is recognized legally, religiously, and socially. The Bible states that marriage is different from all other kinds of deep romantic relations. Marriage is a sacred bond. It is a contract undergirded by serious vows. Matrimony is the most powerful connection after one's connection with the ultimate power. The next thing is to commit to authentic communication.

Authentic communication means to bring who you are to the relationship. Be open about your strengths as well as your weaknesses. In marriage, communication should be genuine and respectful. So, building a marriage on a practical set of true spiritual principles is a secure foundation for a happy, enduring marriage. For example, let us ponder a few biblical principles from the scriptures. The scripture tells us to be kind and affectionate toward each other. Let us learn to treat one another as we desire to be treated and love fervently. In order to convey love in a union, each person must be able to ask for what their needs are in the relationship.

Communication is a big challenge for marital relationships. I have observed that communication challenges are like an unexpected storm. They can arise at any time. Many couples struggle to understand emotional triggers that cause conflict. The daily problems they face are minor. However, when issues are swept under the rug, it causes irreparable damage to the foundation of the relationship.

When couples seek counsel, I can trace most of their conflict back to communication breakdown. My role is to attempt to repair the relationship through reestablishing effective communication. Building good marriage relations will require effort, insight, and determination. So, what are some skill sets that will be needed to establish an enduring happy marriage?

1. Clear communication between the couples is essential. Clear communications mean conveying a message that is clear and concise.
2. Effective communication combines skills, including verbal and nonverbal communication, attentive listening, the ability to manage stress in the moment, and the capacity to understand and recognize your own emotions and the person you are communicating with.

3. Remember that, like any other worthwhile pursuit, learning to be a good communicator in your marriage will be hard, but the rewards will be greater than the efforts.

Marital Challenges

> "I have no way of knowing whether or not you married the wrong person. But I do know that if you treat the wrong person like the right person, you could well end up having married the right person after all. It is far more important to BE the right kind of person than it is to marry the right person."
>
> Zig Ziglar

Have you ever heard someone say I think I married the wrong person? Usually, these words are expressed during moments of conflict, disagreement, or heartbreak. Why do so many allow the challenging circumstances of life to cause them to lose hope in their relationship? I liken relational problems to a blockage in the communicative flow of the relationship.

Sometimes, there are unresolved conflicts blocking the flow and fluidity of healthy communication. Healthy communication is a give-and-take exchange where one feels heard and appreciated. When there is an imbalance of giving and taking, it is a sign that the relational account is in the red. Being in the red with your financial institution is not a good feeling. While some overdrafts could be overturned, too many is a sign of negligence. This concept was discussed by Dr. Gottman. He shed light on the importance of making deposits. He could predict relational success or failure based on the intentional deposits.

When the relational bank account is in the red, the following behaviors manifest: isolation, resentment, bitterness, anger, guilt, shame, regret, despair, and more. Many couples spend years with bottled-up

Identify Relational Problems

resentment. By the time they make it to my office, they are on the verge of exploding. It appears that the feelings have mounted like Mount Rushmore. It is challenging to carve through a mountain of unforgiveness and bitterness. A few years ago, I worked with a middle-aged Jewish couple. They had allowed many Yom Kippurs to pass by; they were gripped by unforgiveness. Even during the holiest holiday of the year, they were not willing to let go of this bitterness.

One of the common trends I have noticed while working with individuals who experience challenges in their marriage is the inability to let go and move forward. When I played professional football, I learned that a key aspect of being a good player is the ability to forget a bad play and move on to the next play. Many times, couples are not willing to move on to the next play in their relationship. They are fuming and fussing over spilled milk.

When counseling couples, I am always curious to hear stories about when individuals first met. Recently, I sat with a couple experiencing communication problems. The tension was swelling, so I reached back into the relationship to times when they first laid eyes on each other. The mood of the room suddenly shifted. It was like the scene of a drama play. They each began to express the joys of when they first met. These moments are often hidden or go unnoticed due to marital challenges.

It is fascinating how the power of language can shift, thinking from negativity or hopelessness to a positive point of view. Beneath the rock pile of problems are gems that need to be dug out. I dig out the gems through authentic communication of true feelings.

I've discovered that unexpressed hurts and pain create toxicity in relationships.

Here are some tips for maintaining healthy relationships.

1. It's better to over-communicate than to allow unmet expectations to pile up.
2. Be a good listener and tune into one's feelings.
3. I recommend repeating what your partner expressed to avoid confusion.
4. Don't go to bed with unresolved conflicts festering.
5. Continue to do the things that you did when you first met.
6. Avoid wearing your feelings on your sleeve and taking things personally.
7. Be a giver in your relationship and not a taker.
8. The simple words "I am sorry" can ease relational hurts and tensions.
9. I encourage couples to find time to pray together. Prayer can change the atmosphere of one's relationship. Don't pray to or at the person. Pray for the relationship's health.

Peer Relationships Problems

Pastor James

Youth of the same age groups are faced with many problems. Teens need discernment and wisdom when making choices about the people whom they can trust. They should find friends who are supportive and trustworthy. Supportive friendships can be hard to find. Choosing friends can be a dangerous proposition. Peers need to be wise in how they open their hearts. Individuals should surround themselves with positive people and say no to negative influences. In some situations, trying to fit in with peers can lead to rejection and damage to one's self-esteem. Strive for growth in life. Resist temptation. Don't desire to walk in the shadows of those teens who may appear popular. As you know, looks can be deceptive. Another huge challenge for many is racism. Peers with racist tendencies are ostracized. Discrimination and demeaning other peers are situations of racism. It arises as a huge challenge to contend with. Therefore, we must inform and empower our youth with insights and tools to resist negative influence resulting from negative peer pressures.

What are some effective ways to deal with peer pressure?
1. Stand up to peers.
2. Tell parents.
3. Report to teachers.
4. Say something to supportive friends.

What do psychologists say about the problems of peer pressure? Psychological research reports that susceptibility to peer pressure begins around adolescence. Adolescents often encourage peers to conform to their behavior. Sometimes peer pressure can be positive, but in many cases, peer pressure is negative. When peer pressure is negative, it can cause many destructive outcomes. For example, a vast number of youths fall into drug addiction because of peer pressure. Peer pressure can cause mental, emotional, and self-esteem problems. Peer pressure is dangerous because it can lead teens into lifelong chronic addictive behaviors. So, a better job must be done in equipping the youth to learn to say no to negative peer pressure. We must raise the awareness of young people. The epidemic perverseness of peer pressure forces peers to conform to the habits of others in their groups.

So, what can one do to not conform to the wayward people's expectations in their midst? The Bible states that you should not conform to those around you but be renewed in the spirit of your mind so that you may prove what is acceptable. Romans 12:2 Peer pressure can make you lose your goals and forget dreams.

The main problem that youths encounter is trying to fit in with peers. I have a great interest in the next generation. In my church, every Sunday morning, I call the children up to give helpful instructions. I give them instructions about choices, peers, and life dreams and goals. I tell them to never drink alcohol, never do drugs, get an education, and put God first. I believe children who have a strong spiritual foundation are safeguarded from traps of negative peer association. While most adolescents have a desire to fit in with peers, my aim in our youth empowerment programs is to give them a desire to identify prosocial peers.

Peer Relationships Problems

Dr. Trahern (Tron)

According to research, U.S. teens ages thirteen to seventeen face anxiety, depression, bullying, and drug and alcohol as major problems (Pew Research Center).

Youths face many challenges. Therefore, it is important to have effective family-based interventions to address the known risks of today's youth. I believe scientific interventions and faith-based principles can better equip our youth to deal with challenges. In addition to my private practice, I facilitate a youth empowerment program dealing with the challenges of today's youth. During sessions, we begin by playing a fun interactive Jeopardy game related to the topic.

Then, I facilitate an interactive session addressing topics such as obeying authority, decision-making, self-esteem, leadership, thinking before you act, self-control, and more. While facilitating these discussions, parents tune in to hear some of the struggles their youth face. Armed with this information, they can increase support for their children.

In scenario 3, George, who is seventeen years old, is facing peer challenges. He lives in the suburbs. He is the youngest of the three. Because of George's history, he is seen as a troubled youth. Everywhere he goes, he is targeted. George feels inferior because of his short and chubby stature. George is struggling academically due to frequent suspensions. He also had an encounter with police due to his association with negative peers.

George's parents, Casey and Charlie, tried everything they could to help George, but nothing worked. He went to many counselors, but there has been no change.

> "Only surround yourself with people who will lift you higher."
>
> — Oprah Winfrey

There are two reasons youth go astray: association with negative peers and a lack of monitoring. I have witnessed many cases like George's. Following, I will provide tips on how to help youth face the challenges that George is facing. Firstly, I would create a plan to strengthen the family system. This is done through searching for strengths as one would mine for gold.

Secondly, I would observe times when youth have positive relationships with their family of origin. When one is treated positively at home, they are less likely to succumb to pressure outside the home. Thirdly, it is important to engage youth in prosocial activities.

Fourthly, youth engage in a positive interaction with their caregivers and siblings daily. Family relationships should be strong, and there should be no name-calling or put-downs in family systems.

Fifthly, I encourage families to have meals together daily or at least three times per week without the distractions of electronics. Lastly, when I was a youth, I used to hear the saying that a family that prays together stays together. I encourage families to strengthen their spiritual muscles through interaction and selfless acts of kindness.

Challenges in Work Relationships

Pastor James

What are some challenges that employees encounter in the workplace? Here are some relationship problems that can stop one from achieving success on the job and in their career.

Low employee engagement, overwhelming workload, and poor communication all lead to frustration. Lack of recognition for excellent work and coworkers' conflict can present a huge problem in the workplace. Team leadership is important in bolstering good morale among workers. Employee training and providing proper tools and resources are vital in dealing with the challenges in the workforce and trusting that the employer will offer fair wages and benefits to the workers will create job satisfaction. It is important to feel that when you give more than is required, your efforts will be noticed and appreciated, promoting a spirited work environment.

The challenge of trusting that all will receive equal recognition for equal work performance. Employers should ensure that minorities have an equal opportunity for promotions and advancement in the marketplace.

The next consideration is what are some effective ways for dealing with workplace challenges? Minorities need to be thoroughly aware of the policies concerning discrimination in the workplace. Where discrimination exists in the workplace, it should be reported to the proper

Identify Relational Problems

authorities. So, when improprieties exist, speak up and speak out.

How to deal with workplace challenges? It is very important that all parties work together to create a caring and friendly atmosphere. Resolve to have each other's back as a unit. Workplace satisfaction promotes all aspects of overall personal well-being for everyone. It can be challenging but rewarding.

The greatest challenge of the workplace environment.

Here are six ways to overcome challenges in the workplace.
1. Speak positively to everyone at all times.
2. A lack of communication and structure can create a challenge.
3. Opportunities to have employees have their voices heard.
4. Competition and personality friction between employees.
5. Ethical issues in the work setting.
6. Workplace gossip.

Observations of what laborers faced in my generation and how we contended with the workplace challenges at that time. We had to survive. Therefore, we had to dig within and meet the workplace challenges of that day. Our only hope was to look for a better day.

In work relationships, pleasing one's boss is always at the forefront of employee relationships. I am from the era of working in the cotton fields of Georgia for little or nothing a day. My father used to work from sunup to sundown for $0.60 a day. The value of hard work was instilled in me. My goal is to instill hard work into the next generation. Therefore, I believe learning how to work well with others is vital. Many years ago, I learned to do my work well. I apply principles of doing my work unto God. Learning to approach work with this mindset enhanced my relationship with my boss and my colleagues. Having a good attitude is everything.

Challenges in Work Relationships

Dr. Trahern (Tron)

As of July 2023, there were 168.35 million individuals in the US labor force (www.statista.com). Since these numbers are vast, it is important to discuss ways for individuals to work effectively in the workforce when challenges are encountered.

Work challenges can be defined as hurdles that hinder goal achievement. While companies have policies and procedures to define company expectations of performance, keeping employees is still a struggle. Some people bounce from job to job like a bunny looking for the best carrot. This can be frustrating for companies who invest much time and energy in their employees. I have been on the receiving end of those resignation emails that affect team morale and productivity. These resignations came as a surprise. However, if I were to look closely at the signs, this individual's word checked out. Perhaps they were quiet quitting. According to the *Harvard Business Review,* these individuals "opt out of tasks beyond one's assigned duties and/or becoming less psychologically invested in work" (Klotz & Mark, "When Quiet Quitting Is Worse Than the Real Thing," 2022).

Data on work satisfaction

Although millions of people go to work daily, only a little over half find their work satisfying and rewarding. Why is there such a disparity in work satisfaction on jobs? Why are so many people dissatisfied? In over a decade of supervising masters-level therapists, I have discovered trends in relationships that affect work satisfaction.

- ☞ Frustrations with colleagues
- ☞ Home life spills over into work life
- ☞ Lack of confidence
- ☞ Resentment
- ☞ Not being a team player
- ☞ Complacency
- ☞ Negative Attitude

In 2015, I conducted a research study of what led an award-winning team to be the top 1% in the world. Data was based on one of the 500 programs in thirty-four states and fifteen countries. This evidence-based program consisted of four therapists, a supervisor, and a program coordinator. My findings and discoveries provided what worked for the therapist on the frontlines of this excellent program. This study showed what works to make this program an award-winning program. The seven factors were 1) togetherness, 2) accolades, 3) feedback, 4) engagement, 5) learning, 6) support, and 7) family support (consumer service or therapy services rendered to families).

As I interviewed each team member, expressions of joy were on their faces. The atmosphere was light and conducive to teamwork. There was a bond that was like glue. They stuck together. The team members had each other's back. There were accolades given for team and individual success. Moreover, there was a healthy peer-to-peer dialogue. Ongoing feedback was provided by the supervisor and program coordinator. Also, there was ongoing training to enhance clinical skills. Excellent customer service was reflected in the therapist's adherence measure surveys given to families.

Here are seven strategies based on my research findings to enhance organizational effectiveness.

1. Togetherness is essential for organizational success. It's important to develop a culture where everyone feels connected to the mission.

2. Accolades were essential for the award-winning team. Staff felt appreciated because of the acknowledgment of their superiors. It's important to find creative ways to acknowledge employees.

3. Feedback is important. Everyone wants to know how well they're doing in their job. I recommend continuous feedback loops and evaluations to enhance effectiveness.

4. Engagement is a critical part of organizational success. We've all seen the joy of a person who may have gotten recently engaged. They are so excited about the journey of love. Likewise, when there is true engagement within organizations, there is passion for the work and motivation to achieve goals.

5. Learning should be continuous. Unfortunately for many, after the initial training, perhaps learning comes to a halt. Let us endeavor to continue to create systems to sustain and maintain competence.

6. Support from one's superior is important in achieving success on the job. Many employees

have stayed committed and faithful to their jobs because of their boss's support.

7. Family support (or consumer service). It's important to hear what the customer is saying about the quality of the services rendered. There should be systems in place to see how well staff connects with customers.

Challenges for Students

Pastor James

It is important to select friends who share common beliefs. Making friends is something that all students desire. While it's challenging to identify authentic friendships, it is vital for one's success in life.

What are some of the biggest challenges that middle school children have to deal with? Entering middle school, children have to carry a heavy academic load. This will require much more discipline and adjustment of time, energy, and other resources. This phase of youth requires a big leap in social adjustment. Making friends and learning peer association and interactions will be one of the greatest challenges for adolescents.

As students enter high school and their first years, they will also face a mountain of challenges.

1. The challenge of making healthy choices.
2. Awareness of the new environment.
3. Peer associations.
4. Wellness agenda.
5. Study habits.
6. Spiritual nourishment.
7. Personal safety.

How to Interact with Peers

Children entering middle school must begin dealing with heavier academics. They must learn to adapt socially and create peer associations. Learn how to resist negative peer associations.

Challenges for Students

Dr. Trahern (Tron)

> "Education is the passport to the future, for tomorrow belongs to those who prepare for it today."
>
> —Malcolm X

While Malcolm X may have held controversial views on certain matters, however, his educational quote speaks volumes. He believed education is the passport to the future of our youth.

Recently, my family and I took a trip out of the country. Prior to traveling, we had to renew our passports because they expired. It was a tedious process, but it was worth it, as we stood in the long lines waiting to gain access to the country in which we were longing to go.

The Malcolm X quote resonates with me because I have witnessed many youths being denied access to a hopeful future because of expired passports or, in some instances, no passport. This means they did not have educational support, and neither did they take advantage of the opportunities to educate themselves. This is disheartening because our fore-parents fought for better educational opportunities for future generations.

Growing up, I used to hear my father say, "Son, if you pay the price now, you can play later; but if you play now, you will pay the price later." These words accompanied me along the path of life. They were the lighthouse to help me stay on course during turbulent times.

Not every child has the support of a parent; many sons and daughters must lie on their pillow, not knowing where their father is. But despite it, they are determined to go on anyhow.

I believe many of our youth are paying the price because they want a better future for themselves. Last week, I met a little boy who achieved Student of the Week after being placed in a shelter. Even though he did not have the support of parents, he excelled academically. I have always been fascinated by the stories of those who have overcome what appeared to be insurmountable odds to achieve excellence in life.

While this is the case for some, others struggle to get their passports. Let's reconsider the above scenario on George. George is seventeen years old. He had run-ins with the law and frequent school suspensions. George always felt inferior because of his short and chubby stature. These feelings led to him seeking approval from negative peers. Sadly, his association with peers led to a path of negative outcomes. Now, he and his parents are paying the price. The wisest men to ever live said, "A child left to him or herself brings shame." I believe this verse is translated as those who lack structure, discipline, guidance, support, nurture, and encouragement want to have a well-adjusted life. In George's case, he lacked support at home because his parents worked all the time.

Let's consider other factors that could be pitfalls for other youths who struggle academically. I have observed that multi-faceted problems contribute to academic challenges. For instance, youth struggle with test anxiety, fear of failure, lack of support, lack of focus, behavioral challenges, family conflict, peer pressure, social media, uncertainty about the future, and an array of other unknown challenges.

Many of these challenges pose difficulty in obtaining a passport to future success. I believe one can climb the mountain of success through proper treatment and guidance along with other values such as determination, diligence, hard work, and faith.

For the remainder of this chapter, I will recommend a treatment plan that would help George overcome the challenges that he faces. Perhaps others can glean insight from this plan to help your youth achieve success.

1. Identify the problem.
2. Create an action plan.
3. Identify the key players within the family system, home, community, school, and work collaboratively.
4. In the role, George is in a desired activity. This may require some probing, but it is possible.
5. Fill in the gaps of all unstructured time. Unstructured time can lead to an idle mind.
6. Connect George's family to a faith-based community to inspire hope. This step is important because there are many people within faith-based organizations who have been overcomers. And they are willing to inspire others with their stories of hope.
7. Connecting George to a mentor, coach, teacher, or other support will help inspire him.
8. Connect him with tutoring services and mentoring.

9. Community service for restitution.

While every youth faces different challenges, George's action plan is a lens providing insight into ways to overcome difficulties that youth may face. While there is no one-size-fits-all solution, there are proven strategies that can help youth to obtain academic success.

Chapter 2

What Causes Division in Relationships?

What Causes Division in Relationships?

Pastor James

When closeness has been lost in family relationships, what can we do? Pray to God and ask for peace, courage, and wisdom on how to bring restoration to your relationships.

The lack of understanding may be one of the great contributors to disconnection in relations. This causes families to stop sharing thoughts, feelings, and time with each other. This is true for all types of relationships. The closeness bond will perish when there is a lack of communication and understanding. The lack of communication and insight will lead to distrust, anger, hurt, and disconnect. When this happens, both parties can be left hurt and misunderstood. What can be done to mend these damaged feelings? One must reach out to the member of the family who feels hurt. Speak to the distressed person with empathy. The best strategy is to take the humble approach in order to give the relation a chance to work. Act as a sounding board, and discuss your ideas with them. Mirror what is being said by reflecting what they are saying to you in a compassionate way.

It is stated in *Family Today* that breakdown in family relations can arise from beliefs, unresolved traumas, and unbalanced emotional strength, ill health, and jealousy among family members, which can cause long-term disconnect. The key is to try to bring partners or family back together. Regardless of what caused the drift, we need each other. The Creator made us this way. So, what can we do?

Relationships that we have invested in are worth saving. This may require training and hard work, but the rewards will be worth the effort. We should pray fervent prayers about the issues of divide. Honest petition to the Creator asking for discernment and wisdom for starting the healing process in a loving way. This willingness to stand down can bridge the gap in relationships. However, you will need to take care of your own emotions. What are some effective steps that can be taken to help broken families come closer?

- ☞ Practice kindness by showing genuine concern and understanding.
- ☞ Agree to communicate by clearly stating a desire to work toward mending relationships.
- ☞ Write respectful letters that talk about the value of coming closer together.
- ☞ Seek professional spiritual counseling.

"Most of the problems in life are because we act without thinking, or we keep thinking without acting."

Zig Ziglar

Things happen in life that are difficult to deal with. It is our God-given duty to strive to solve problems.

Problems call for a solution. They are challenges of real concern that need a solution. Problems are something hard to deal with. When issues are difficult or impossible to solve, turn them over to the Creator through prayer. When problems are too big for you to handle, make the Serenity Prayer your motto. Pray "God, grant me the serenity to accept the things that I cannot change, the courage to change the things that I can, and the wisdom to know the difference"… Problems can be viewed as a test of character. They can build character. Problems are to be solved, not to run away from. As the saying goes, we may need to grab the bull by the horns. Test yourself to see if you are mature enough to wade through the issues you are facing. If not, go to the Highest Power in fervent prayer. Ask for divine direction. Make a decision to start anew.

What if you get out of bed every day and shout, "This is the day that the Lord has made; I will rejoice and be glad in it"? Then, make it a practice to always put your best foot forward. Be determined that you are going to be a difference-maker in all your relationships. Determine that you will strive to make a difference in your marriage and in all your blood relationships. Work on the issues that seem to be pushing the family members apart. Pray for insights on the matters that cause conflict in the family unit.

The Holy Scriptures have always been the bedrock source of love and healing or restoration of the family. But the enduring principles must be diligently applied to the cause of the divide in your relations.

There are many issues that can cause divides in families. However, the primary cause of conflicts in the family is differences in opinions and favoritism. The best boundaries, support, and reinforcers come from the teachings of scripture. Let us consider some insights for closing the gaps and disconnects in family structure.

1 Corinthians 1:10 says "Now I beech you, brethren, by the Lord Jesus Christ, that ye all speak the same thing, that there be no division among you be perfectly joined together in the same mind and the same judgment." The aforementioned quotation points to the kind of spiritual connection that can inspire believers to work toward keeping peace and harmony among each other. They are commanded to work out differences, affections, and understanding, Be a helpmate to one another in love. So, what can we do about starting the process of repairing the brokenness that exists in far too many families? Don't hesitate to seek counsel from a competent therapist or pastoral counselor.

What Causes Division in Relationships?
Dr. Trahern (Tron)

We live in a world where there is much division. There is division in many areas of society politically, educationally, spiritually, and culturally. I believe these divisions have spilled over into interpersonal relationships within families. The inability to get along with others is causing havoc in our interpersonal relationships. For over a decade, I have watched parents in conflict with their children. I have witnessed the fabric of marital relationships torn apart, and I have seen friendships dissolve.

Let's revisit the four challenges discussed in the scenarios. These challenges are not uncommon. Many have experienced broken relationships, jealousy, resentment, marital challenges, challenges raising children, and challenges as one advances in age.

In scenario one, Nancy and Mike have been married for many years. They are raising four children. But Nancy feels slighted because her sacrifice to leave her business career to be a stay-at-home mother is not being appreciated. As a result, resentments are mounting. Mike, who was once the love of her life, does not know what to do. He feels he does not get any empowerment for being the breadwinner. As a matter of fact, Nancy can be careless about his breadwinner title because she made more than him before leaving her six-figure salary to stay home. During the argument, she even told him he needed to make more money. This wrestling match of words has created division. Now, they are sleeping in separate rooms, which they vowed not to do.

In scenario two, Tiffany (twenty-two years old) and Felicity (twenty-one years old) used to have a close bond, but over time their relationship has become strained. It all started when Tiffany felt that Felicity was getting more attention from their parents. Sadly, the unresolved feelings have spilled over into adulthood. I have witnessed countless parents lavish praise on one child while the other child receives crumbs of encouragement. These pent-up emotions can lead to outbursts and destructive entitlements. Even though Tiffany tried to mask and push down the pain, in later years, it started to come out. It was like a broken dam that needed to be repaired.

In scenario three, a youth (George) is seventeen years old. His suburban home and the success of his parents were not enough to keep him from engaging in crime and negative peer association. His choice to forgo his academics has led to resentment in the family relationships. The parents hoped that he would have taken advantage of the opportunities that they didn't have, but regrettably, he took another path because of the emotional pain he was experiencing.

In scenario four, Myles is a retired schoolteacher. After thirty years of teaching students in the inner city, he became depressed because of a recent doctor's visit. Unhealthy habits have caught up with him. The physician is recommending that Myles become more active; if not, he will become diabetic. Myles feels overwhelmed and does not know what to do. He has no family support.

Given the above scenarios, one of the main causes of division in relationships (family, siblings, and friends) is differences in beliefs and decision-making. When values are not aligned, relationships go off course. To illustrate this point, think of a vehicle. A person could have four brand-new tires. But if they are not aligned, it will impact the tires. They will soon wear out. Likewise, learning communication skills and techniques is not enough. One must be aligned emotionally, and I recommend spiritually to establish a foundation for a healthy relationship.

In the above scenarios, counseling is necessary to repair the relationships. In the sacred writings of scripture, it says without a foundation, what can the righteous do? This means even if you are a good person, without a strong foundation, there can be no lasting success.

Relational Divisions

I believe relational division occurs due to a lack of shared values. For instance, when working with couples and intimate partners, I observed that a lack of shared values causes dissonance. Relationships would be better if values aligned. In my work, conflict happens because of differences in belief systems. When I sit down with families who experience division, I aim to help them find commonalities. My first step as a pastor is to get them to believe in God. I believe this is the foundation for all secure attachments.

What Causes Relational Imbalances in Relationship Systems?

Pastor James

People are complicated, but we have an innate need for each other. So, we must lift up one another in love. We all desire to have great relationships, but excellent relationships must be built. They don't automatically happen. It takes hard work. We must identify and root out issues that cause disconnection.

Let's look at issues that can cause detachment within the family structure. Emotional patterns can be problematic when creating balance in relationships. We need to do everything that we can possibly do to bring equilibrium to all our relationships. We need to recognize the impact of negative feelings and how they affect our relations.

The first step is to open communication and dialogue about the emotional baggage that has caused the family to drift apart. Reach out to family and friends and ask for a family gathering. It is essential to start the process. Family systems are dynamic processes. So, what are some of the dilemmas in the family system that have created disharmony in the group? Where there is a lack of moral and ethical values, disharmony will prevail. How can a family system be defined? It is good to seek knowledge about the sensitive parts of the family unit.

When any group of people shares a common identity or purpose (this can mean families, partners, siblings, vocations, and religion), such is considered a family unit. All family systems are very important. All our relationships will need investment. Suppose that every person put in their best effort to enrich their relationships. The world would be a better place if everyone would put a premium on the betterment of their personal relations. We can do this. The question is where we start. Without knowledge and wisdom, relationships will not grow. They are like plants; you must cultivate them. Learn to do things to help the relationship grow and flourish. Pray together. Be honest with each other. Keep an open mind. Seek mentoring from those who have learned about family enrichment. How does the family system work?

Let us start with the meaning of family systems intelligence. Family systems is a theory. It is designed to comprehend human functioning that emphasizes establishing the connections between family members. Bowens views the family as a living system whose relationships are interconnected. The goal is to breed into each person the relationships in a way to breed into each individual cooperation, respect, and kindness.

Family Systems means are energized by emotional, psychological, and social factors; it is a very complex and dynamic institution. Creating balance among the members will always be countered by strong resistance. According to the model, family systems are a group of people who interact with each other mutually with positive energy. All the people are a key part of the system and are vitally connected. Any part in the system belongs to each other. And this creates equal exchanges among them. One of the primary functions it provides is a foundation for building a strong legacy of social and spiritual qualities. There are no perfect families. Every family has conflict, challenges, and issues. But families can be good and strong. 1 Timothy 5:8 But if any man provided not for his family, he is worse than an infidel.

Relational means dealing with many types of relationships. Dealing with overbearing family members and developing a relationship with needy people in relations will depend on the approach to how to help the system. It pays to search for ways of bringing equity to relations. Be willing to go out of your way to engage the family members on inherent values, bringing the family closer. There are many simple things that all members can do to help establish a positive foundation in the system.

Power dynamics and conflicts can build up or tear down relationships. They can create harmony or conflict. These roles interact so as to influence behavior in unhealthy ways. What are some of the imbalances that happen in families? One person may receive more praise and approval than other members. Some individuals may be more talented than others in the family. How can we overcome them? What causes the imbalances in family relations? Encourage family members to stand up for each other. Support each other.

Relational imbalances are like a balance sheet. When there is fairness in relationships, balance occurs. But unfairness creates debts. For example, when a child feels that a parent favors a sibling, unfairness happens. The child who was treated unfairly may believe that the parents owe him. These dynamics create relational imbalances.

For example, let us consider some of the disunity that often occurs among siblings.

In sibling relations, what can cause division? When a sibling feels that he or she has been treated unfairly, this causes emotional difficulty. When immature parents show favoritism to one child over another, it can lead to anger and resentment in the family system. Fairness, equality, and trust are essential in all relationships. If cooperation is not a shared experience, the relationship will be rocky. The good news is that all concerned individuals can learn to bring healing and value to all of their relations. Bring victory to romance, marriage, siblings, finances, spirituality, jobs, and a better relationship with yourself. What are some tips that can be effective for the enrichment of all relations?

What Causes Division in Relationships?

Use the methods listed below religiously as a treatment for improving your relationships. The requirement for success is to put forth your best effort in the application of spiritual principles. Spirituality are those enduring principles. The principles listed below are enduring principles. They have been tested.

1. Pray for divine guidance. Ask God for leading.
2. Make a decision to take action. Do something to solve problems in your relationships.
3. Have honest and open communication.

What Causes Relational Imbalances in Relationship Systems?

Dr. Trahern (Tron)

The best way to illustrate relational imbalances is to think of a balancing scale. If everything is equal, there will be balance, but if one side is weighed down, imbalance occurs. In my work as a family therapist, I have learned that trust is a necessary ingredient in families when imbalances and injustices affect closeness and harmony. Perhaps we all have experienced relationship breakdowns because of a lack of fairness and caring. Sadly, these conflicts spill over into all our relationships and affect multiple generations.

The goal is to restore people's capacity to love, show fairness, and build trust. This is easier said than done. When people have pent-up emotions, it can affect their marriage, sibling relationships, and academics and spill over into later years.

Division in Family Relationships

Pastor James

Real closeness is about truth. *You shall know the truth, and the truth shall set you free.* John 8:32

The main cause of division in family relations is likely a lack of honest communication. Communication is key to all relationships because it allows you to get your feelings out. Share the good and bad. Share the hurt and the joy. It will bring you closer.

When you talk about how you are feeling with your partner, this permits an opportunity for solving the issues. You can become a better problem solver through good communication. Effectual communication can prevent painful arguments. Aways speak to your companion in a kind, respectful way. Open communication can serve as a pathway for seeking professional and spiritual help for answers.

Family counseling can help strengthen the bonds in your family relationships. Family counselors can help couples and family members identify problems and offer insight on how to solve their differences and difficulties. Family counselors help the members look at patterns of behaviors that may be rooted in past generations and may be parts of the present.

The counselor brings education, training, and experience to the session. This all serves to help the group gain knowledge and insights toward mending brokenness in their relationships. Good spiritual counseling can also offer effective healing balms to troubled relationships. There is a passage in Psalms chapter 1 that offers wisdom about the benefit of spiritual counseling.

Division in Family Relationships

Dr. Trahern (Tron)

Why does division occur in family relationships? In my work as a marriage and family therapist, I have identified three primary reasons why division happens in relationships. Number one, there is a lack of trust. When trust is broken in families, the bond is broken. Number two, unresolved conflict. I have observed countless families carrying baggage from the past. The inability to express emotional injuries leads to resentment. Resentments can cause a break in marital, sibling, and other intimate relationships. Number three, there is a lack of faith. I believe God created families, and for relationships to work, God needs to be interwoven in the relationship system.

Dating

Pastor James

Core values are values that are the essential elements for building a solid relationship. Good, lasting relations require shared values. When you are looking to find a lasting bond, the first thing is to sit down and write a long list of the kinds of values that you would desire to share with a partner. Start with the alignment of your beliefs and your faith. Start with a principled-based courtship; try to keep the dating process respectful. Don't compromise your principles. Don't try to impress your partner. Be honest about who you are. Spend quality time together. Get to know the parents when possible.

Pay careful attention to your core values. Be aware of how well you communicate together. Take notice of whether you truly enjoy each other's company. Do you laugh a lot? If you are open and positive, do not choose a person who has a negative disposition. Remember that the Bible says not to be unequally yoked. Search for similar enduring values.

Dating

Dr. Trahern (Tron)

Dating is an important step in building a healthy and lasting relationship. I define dating as two people getting to know each other in the hope of establishing a lasting relationship.

To illustrate, if one were to undertake the task of building a home, proper building material would be sought out to complete the project. In the establishment of a lasting relationship, one must seek out essential core building blocks to establish a healthy and lasting relationship. I have discovered that love, respect, commitment, loyalty, communication, authenticity, kindness, forgiveness, and faith are key building blocks for a relationship.

Sadly, many undertake the task of dating with little insight as to what it takes to make a relationship work. In counseling, one of the questions I often ask as an assessment question is, have you ever seen a healthy relationship? Over half of my clients struggle to identify individuals they know who have a healthy relationship. Perhaps you feel the same way; there are not enough healthy relationships modeled in our society. Many relationships are built on shallow materials that are unable to withstand the conflicts one will face in life. Relational challenges are a normal part of relationships; however, when the foundation is not secure, one is likely to renege on one's promise.

Therefore, it is essential to get off to a good start when one begins the dating process. I recommend writing down some essential values during the early stage of your dating and comparing notes to see if you and your partner are on the same page. If you're not on the same page, perhaps that's a red flag or a stop sign that you don't need to proceed further.

Division in Marriage Relationships

Pastor James

The primary cause of division in marriage is financial problems. When there is not enough money to support a decent lifestyle in the marriage, problems in the relationship begin to arise. First, there must be an ability or skills to earn a sufficient decent way of life. A second issue that can rip apart a marriage is the silent treatment.

According to *Medical News Today*, silent treatment means that one is not openly communicating what is bothering them. It is when one partner deliberately avoids talking to the other party. This kind of act is very toxic to a marriage. This strategy causes anger. Another primary cause of problems in marriage arises when a partner refuses to let go of an accusation and keeps repeating it over and over. It is also very harmful to keep looking for the negative side to every issue in a relationship. Too much complaining is inexpedient. Make compatible values a must when seeking to build a good marriage. Faithfulness: Be fully committed to your partner forever. Friendship in marriage is a shared intention to be together as long as life shall last. This is life's most cemented union outside of one's union with God. Friendship helps married couples feel safe enough to be more open without worrying about being judged or insecure (www.Psychcentral.com).

Friendship must be an essential element of marriage. What does friendship look like in a marriage bond? Mutual respect, tolerance, support, and having each other's back.

Wisdom to resolve conflict keeps hope alive.

Guiding Principles: Trust in God. Faith in God. Continue to nourish and cultivate intimacy in the relationship. Have fun and do lots of things together. Always make time for weekly dates. Work hard on keeping your marriage flourishing. According to *Health Encyclopedia*, the key to a good marriage is work, love, responsibility, and respect. Good marriages don't just happen; both partners must put in the work. What can be done to promote closeness in in-law relationships? Set boundaries. Boundaries are lines that you set in a relationship. These are the limits set that the in-laws are not allowed to cross.

There are rules to keep in-laws out of your personal business. Beware that in-laws can be toxic and controlling. Controlling in-laws try to get the son or daughter to listen to them rather than you. Sometimes, in-laws can become angry and even threatening. Therefore, the best policy is to agree to keep in-laws out of personal matters in your marriage. What are some effective ways of getting along with in-laws? According to WikiHow, be friendly, cordial, and natural around them. Always put your marriage first. Be honest and open around them.

1. Stick to mutual topics.

2. Enforce healthy boundaries.
3. Don't have expectations.
4. Prepare yourself mentally.
5. Don't confront them.

What causes marital division? Marital division happens when couples have different beliefs. To begin, the right individuals must share similar values. For over forty years, I began my counseling sessions by identifying core values. I believe relationships will sink if values are not intact. I remember sitting with a couple in premarital counseling. The mother had a child from a previous relationship. The groom-to-be held the baby during the session. We discussed the future of their marriage. They both had a sparkle in their eyes. But everything changed in the instant when we discussed family responsibilities. I told the young man, "When you marry this woman, you must take full responsibility for her and play a father role for this child." Immediately, he gave the child back to the mother. His response appeared automatic and unconscious. His behavior illustrated a point. They did not share values in co-parenting. I imagine countless couples begin relationships without discussing co-parenting, finances, in-law relationships, families of origin beliefs, and many other important aspects of relationships. Failure to align could be disastrous.

Division in Marriage Relationships

Dr. Trahern (Tron)

> "There is no more lovely, friendly, and charming relationship, communion, or company than a good marriage."
>
> — Martin Luther

Why is it that so many relationships begin with bliss but end in brokenness? Why does the sun rise to the joy of a hopeful future on a wedding day, but for many, the sun sets on feelings of hopelessness? When it comes to marriage, I am biased. I am aware that statistically, nearly 50% of relationships end in divorce (www.forbes.com). But my hope is that 100% of the couples I see will overcome the struggles of heartbreak and leave my office healed.

While this is wishful thinking, the reality is many people find it impossible to work through some of the challenges they face. I've seen the remnants of betrayal, mistrust, and heartbreak.

While I agree with Martin Luther 's premise that there's no more lovely, friendly, and charming relationship, communion, or company than a good marriage, many don't experience these qualities. Perhaps they start out this way, but the feelings soon fade away. What happens? I believe it can be illustrated through what I call a relational garden. There's nothing more beautiful than a well-planted and cultivated garden blooming on a summer day.

Many relationships start out blooming, but over time, due to neglect, overgrown weeds grow. What was once a beautiful rose garden turns into overgrown weeds. For over a decade, I've seen people neglect well-planted gardens. They allow intruders to break down the walls of their garden. Others have allowed the cares of life to lead to negligence of their well-planted garden. Solution-focused therapy says we stopped doing the things that we used to do in our relationships. This means if one began to make those investments again, the relationship would get better. I've seen this strategy work for many couples on the brink, but sadly, I've seen couples who allowed themselves to go over the edge.

So here are some strategies to help improve your relationship:

1. Identify what causes the relational imbalance.
2. Forgive grievances of the past.
3. Express your relational needs.
4. Be a good listener instead of preparing to respond. Listen with an open mind and open heart.
5. Identify what works and keep doing it in your relationship.
6. Put first things first and prioritize what's most important. I have seen people invest more in their pets than their spouses.
7. Let the past be the past. Stop bringing up things from the past; it is not easy, but the alternative is you are sinking your relationship by rehashing things of old.

8. Don't wait too late to seek professional help. For instance, when we feel physical ailments, we go to the doctor; likewise, when we experience relational turbulence and see signs of seeking professional help, we go to the doctor. Don't go to the wrong sources.
9. The bonus is to pray together. I grew up hearing the saying a family that prays together stays together. I would say a couple that prays together lengthens days together. Make it a habit to get on your knees every day and ask God to guide your relationship. I have been practicing this technique for almost fourteen years, and it works wonders for me, Norlene, and our sons.
10. Develop a mission statement about what you want the legacy to be for your relationship.
11. Show gratitude; be thankful for the little things.

Division in In-Law Relationships

Pastor James

In-law relationships: how can they be defined? Look for healthy ways of dealing with in-laws. According to WikiHow, don't engage in arguments since that can quickly turn into bitterness toward you. Always be calm and assertive. Put your marriage first. Set and enforce healthy boundaries. Let go of expectations. Do not confront your in-laws. Hear each other out with love and compassion. Be empathetic with in-laws. Understand what leads to friction in in-law relationships. Seek to be unselfish in how you interact with your in-laws. Allow your differences to bring you closer, not divide you. Communicate your boundaries and expectations in a clear way. When in-laws can connect to the nuclear family in a positive way, it creates a beneficial bond. Positive in-laws can help the family in many practical ways. They can help with the children and provide emotional support.

What causes a rift or division in in-law relationships? Rifts between in-laws and parents occur because of multiple reasons; drinking and other maladies can lead to problems. In my experience of working with families, I've noticed that boundaries are an issue. This shows us the way families interact with each other. When parents or grandparents go beyond boundaries, it creates conflict. In addition to boundary violations, there are also issues of jealousy or problems such as power and control that cause grandparents to go beyond boundaries. When there is relational interference, various problems can arise.

Division in In-Law Relationships

Dr. Trahern (Tron)

> So that there may be no division in the body, but that the members may have the same care for one another.
>
> 1 Corinthians 12:25

What causes division in in-law relationships? To illustrate this point, I will use the metaphor of driving a vehicle. The experience of driving gives a sense of freedom and independence. On a highway, there are many lanes. All lanes serve a purpose and function. Let's apply this concept to marriage. A marriage has a lane. Healthy couples understand their lane's pace and don't drift. The in-laws also have a lane, but when there are unruly in-laws, they cut in and out of their children's lane.

Perhaps in-laws drift out of their lane when they give unwelcome advice or impose their parenting styles on their adult children. Recently, I was conversing with a woman who was visiting her son out of state for her vacation. He is married, and they have two children. When I asked about her time visiting her grandchildren, she gave a sigh of relief. She went on to say she had to get back home. Upon further inquiry, I learned that her urgency to return happened because she couldn't bear to watch her son and daughter-in-law parent. It seemed like the children were running the house. There was an apparent flexibility and lack of structure. By the look of frustration, I could see how her rigidity and no-nonsense parenting style were a clash.

Here are some common challenges I have observed with in-laws imposing their views on their children's family system. Not embracing the spouse of an adult child. Not approving of decisions in child rearing, finances, and other life matters.

Additionally, unresolved conflict between parents and children can also cause communication challenges. Communication that should be a flow is like a traffic jam. When this happens, feelings of resentment occur. But when everybody can stay in their lane, this helps the family system work smoothly.

Division in Sibling Relationships

Pastor James

There are four primary reasons why division happens in sibling relationships. Favoritism, jealousy, quarrels, and squabbles are issues that contribute to division in sibling relationships.

What is the cause of sibling rivalry?

Sibling rivalry happens in families because of competition in family relationships between brothers and sisters. It occurs among blood-related relatives and those not related to each other in various relationships. This competitiveness shows up especially when siblings spend a lot of time growing up together, which could be a contributing factor to rivalry. Additionally, differences in personalities also contribute to division in sibling relationships. In my experience as a Christian counselor, I've observed how personalities impact relationships and influence how families interact with each other. Also, order of birth can cause division because a parent may favor a child because of the rank (first born) of their birth. Parental bias also creates favoritism in sibling relationships, contributing to division. As a result, jealousy and envy often arise. In addition, labeling and teasing can also lead to feelings of anger and resentment in sibling relationships.

Another definition of sibling rivalry is the inability to effectively interact with each other.

But one can improve in their ability to navigate social situations more productively. How can this happen? First, one must develop the skills of paying attention to personal temperament and body language. When this skill is developed, it can be helpful in decreasing division among siblings. Additional factors that contribute to sibling rivalry are experienced in large families. For instance, I grew up in a family of ten. I was the oldest and responsible for my younger siblings. There were times of competition in our relationships. We also had challenging times trying to get our basic needs met, which led to competition.

As siblings, our paths may change as life goes along, but the bond between us will remain forever. Stand up for your brother. You are your brother's keeper. It is right to go after brotherly love. We should always be guided by the Higher Power when it comes to loving our brother. Seek guidance on how to keep the family together. Allow nothing to keep you apart.

What are some effective steps that can help bring siblings together? According to the American Psychological Association (APA), there are key strategies for creating closeness among divided siblings.

1. Do not force your children to share everything with their siblings, but try to offer good opportunities for peaceful resolutions.

2. Consider the other party's points of view.
3. Healthy boundaries allow a person to form close, safe, and trusting relationships while staying true to their own values. (Positive psychology)
4. Forgiveness, humbling ourselves, serving our siblings, and becoming more patient.
5. Come together in meetings.
6. Don't point fingers or look for blame.
7. Refrain from criticizing each other.
8. Try to find the root cause of the problem.
9. Work on the emotions that may be damaging the relationship.
10. Search for strategies that help to overcome emotions that damage relationships.

For the remainder of this book, we will point out how to bridge the gap in relationships. Listed below are several tips, insights, and strategies for assisting you in the repair of estranged relationships.

1. Be understanding.
2. Resolve to be forgiving at all costs.
3. Work at closing the gap in divided relations.
4. Endeavor to strengthen family bonds.
5. Be willing to stand down in order to make peace. Peace is an essential building block of love.

Division in Sibling Relationships

Dr. Trahern (Tron)

Sibling relationships are a vital aspect of a family system. There is a myriad of sibling dynamics in the family. There are siblings who have the same birth parents, adoptive siblings, and blended families. In reflection on my work with siblings, I see a wide range of emotions around this topic. For over a decade, I have been privileged to help families repair relationships. I have gone into homes and witnessed siblings working together effectively. Conversely, I have observed conflict. The conflict looks like an intense game of tug-of-war. Sadly, many youths don't play by the rules. They name-call, put down, insult, and split parents. What causes division and conflict in families?

Conflict dates to siblings who had a conflict that ended tragically. In the Bible, there is a story of two brothers, Cain and Abel. They were the first sons of Adam and Eve. Cain was a farmer who worked in the fields, while Abel was a shepherd who cared for the family's animals. When the time came to present an offering to God, Abel offered the best offering, but Cain offered fruit of the ground. When this happened, jealousy entered their relationship. Cain got so angry with his brother that he murdered him.

Perhaps this is an extreme example, but the reality is that jealousy enters many sibling relationships.

Like a parent who favors a child for doing what is right, God showed favor to Abel, so Cain became angry. This is the moment where division occurred. It happened when Cain realized his brother was accepted, and he was rejected. I believe the division between Abel and Cain stemmed from jealousy.

Here are some tips to overcome emotions that damage sibling relationships:

1. Are there any unresolved conflicts from the past?
2. Let go of hurt feelings.
3. If possible, tell your parents how you feel about being compared to your sibling.
4. Work hard at making amends.
5. Don't bring up hurt once it has been forgiven.
6. Reach out to your siblings once per week.
7. Have family gatherings one to two times per year where everyone is present.
8. Be a good listener.
9. Then, become a peacemaker.
10. See a spiritual advisor or counselor if conflicts appear unresolvable.

Chapter 3

Loving Yourself

Loving Yourself

Pastor James

Self-love is defined as love of self or regard for one's own happiness or advantage and has been conceptualized by the drive and desire to protect and take care of yourself. What is the measure of loving oneself? It is said that the dynamic power of love sent out into the tiniest cell causes light and love. If you love God, yourself, and others, you will not have low self-esteem. If you have high self-esteem, you will be able to achieve more.

According to *Country Living*, happiness begins with loving yourself every beautiful inch, no matter what anyone else thinks. You must make forgiving yourself a prime concern. Tenderness toward yourself promotes personal growth. Julia Terry Roberson said: always build yourself up. Do not engage in anything that will tear you down. Some tips will help you build self-esteem in a better way. What are some of the ingredients for enriching the culture and foundation of the family structure?

According to WikiHow, here are some action steps: reading a book, going for a walk, taking in positive affirmations, eating healthy, praying and meditation, and getting proper sleep. Focus on the kind of interactions that help you to feel good about yourself. According to the Bible, we are commanded to love ourselves. We need to cultivate a richer sense of self-love and family love.

Start honoring yourself for any small accomplishment. The first thing is that we must begin the process of learning to love ourselves. Identify the deficient character issues that hinder the ability to love yourself authentically.

"Love yourself first and everything else will fall into line. You really have to learn how to love yourself in order to get anything done."

Lucille Ball

How can a person start to love themself and teach others to love? Firstly, recognize the lack of love that you hold against yourself. Then, determine that you are going to invest in finding true love for yourself. Decide that you are going to seek and explore the criteria for creating a love relationship with yourself. Loving yourself is not prideful.

Secondly, start with honest and heartfelt prayer. Ask God for help and guidance on how to go about the enrichment process of loving yourself.

Thirdly, seek out some useful tips for enhancing the equality of the love that you have for yourself. Make it a constant practice.

Self-love is contained in the first and greatest commandment in the Bible. I have discovered that self-love is essential in life because it builds self-esteem. It also helps individuals to lead a more inspiring and fulfilling life.

Loving Yourself

Dr. Trahern (Tron)

The maxim "know thyself" has a variety of meanings. In the context of relationships, it means to know your worth. How does one discover their worth amidst the challenges and difficulties of life? In our case example, we discussed Tiffany. She felt like an outcast in her family. She lived in isolation or depression. And she was struggling and failing in her work life. As a result, Tiffany was referred to counseling to discover solutions to her problem. If counseling did not work, she would be in jeopardy of losing her job. Tiffany believed hidden emotions from her youth were manifesting, causing her to crash in her personal and professional life. Perhaps, looking from the outside, a person who did not understand trauma might ask how a woman could allow unresolved conflicts to impact her life.

How to address lack of love in therapy?

If Tiffany came to my practice, I would create space for her to share her story. Then, I would apply family therapy interventions to treat the family relationships that were contributing to these hidden emotions. For instance, instead of focusing on her being estranged from her family, I would focus on the times, even if small, when she had the relationship she desired with her parents and siblings. I would also identify times when she was not having an outburst on her job. In essence, I would help her identify the times when she was being the person she desired to be, meaning having known herself. To illustrate, suppose we compare

Felicity's life to the erection of a strong building structure. For the purposes of explaining, let's call her emotions of jealousy, resentment, anger, and past emotional injuries her foundation. What happens over time when the pressure of life is on Tiffany? Her structure would crumble, meaning her life would fall apart. My aim would be to help her discover her true self.

I have experienced countless individuals whose foundations are not solid because they are not intentional about building on things that will not collapse. Over the years, I have observed abiding principles that have worked for relationship building. Those who build their lives on faith in God, love, and hope last.

What Does It Mean to Love Yourself?

Pastor James

Loving yourself means knowing your needs. When one loves themselves, they know their needs and have come to the knowledge of who they are at the core. In order to love yourself, you must first recognize that you are a spiritual being.

Loving yourself means to have an awareness that you need a strength bigger than yourself. Loving yourself means continuing to work on your spiritual, mental, emotional, and physical development.

The Pathway to Self-Love

Self-love is a pathway. It is illustrated in one who takes a life journey. At the entrance of the door to the pathway is the realization of the need for self-love. The path of self-love is where one discovers and rediscovers one's personal needs. This is a process of determination. It is determining that you are somebody and you have eternal value. Through this awareness, one makes the decision to build a foundation of wellness.

Therefore, loving oneself is a process of engaging in self-care. Self-care is practicing self-acceptance. When we truly love ourselves, we will find time to replenish ourselves.

Loving oneself requires focusing on strengths, not weakness.

What are some practical ways to love ourselves? One, we must forget about our weaknesses and past mistakes. Two, we must practice forgiveness of self. Three, we must move forward in a forgiving way. Four, get rid of negative self-talk. Five, get away from negative people. Six, identify your negative feelings and don't give way to bad feelings or thoughts. Seven, study positive spiritual information.

Finally, we must commit to lots of prayer. When we practice these steps and meditate regularly, we can discover the pathway to loving oneself. I have found these steps to be useful in my own life. I have a routine of staying in touch with nature. I go for regular walks and exercise often. These practices help me both spiritually and emotionally.

What Does It Mean to Love Yourself?
Dr. Trahern (Tron)

To love oneself is to have a healthy self-concept. To have a healthy concept, one must truly appreciate their own uniqueness. When a person has an awareness of their own God-given abilities, talents, gifts, and skills, they can avoid rejection of self. I believe that for a person to truly love others, they must be able to love God and themselves. When one lacks in the area of loving themselves, they feel inferior to other people. Feeling inferior, they try to get in other people's lanes in life. This means one is always comparing oneself to others, and one never has enough depth to realize their own giftedness. A favorite quote that sheds light on one uniqueness is Henry David Thoreau's statement in *Walden* (1854): "If a man does not keep pace with his companions, perhaps it is because he hears a different drummer."

Perhaps we need to celebrate our own uniqueness and have an appreciation for the gifts that we have been given rather than compare ourselves to other people. This will help us to have a greater love for ourselves.

Finding True Love

Pastor James

True love is unconditional love. It is a feeling of care and concern for others. How does one find it? It begins with the individual. I believe we cannot give something we have not possessed.

True love is a reciprocal process. It is said when you intend something, the universe will work for you. If we want to discover the depths of true love, we must be desperate enough to seek the prime mover of the universe. He will help us to find it.

Finding True Love

Dr. Trahern (LaFavor)

How do we find true love? It has been written in the Bible that "God is love" (1 John 4:8). Since God is love, those who find Him find true love. But how does one find God? I believe God is found when one makes up one's mind to pursue Him wholeheartedly. When we search for Him as one mines for gold, we will find Him. Those who mine gold use proper machinery, which helps them to adequately drill wide and deep. Likewise, when we search for God, we must use tools of faith. Faith helps us believe that God exists. The ancient writer in Hebrews said, "But without faith it is impossible to please Him, for he who comes to God must believe that He is, and that He is a rewarder of those who diligently seek Him."

For over a decade, I have witnessed the transforming power of love in therapy. The trained therapist provides a supportive environment that allows patients to talk openly about the challenges of life in a fair, unbiased, and nonjudgmental space.

Discovering the Journey of Love

Pastor James

Let us get started on the path by affirming the goal of true love. How to go about finding true love? We must devote ourselves to loving one another as we love ourselves. To illustrate, athletes must practice perfecting their skills. Therefore, love is a practice that must be engaged in daily. Make expressing love a continuous practice. Work on building being honest and authentic in the love relationships you are trying to find.

Ask yourself what kind of love relationship will give you fulfillment and make you happy?

I believe we must associate with those who possess what we desire. Therefore, hang out with individuals who want the same things you want out of life. There is a saying, know thyself. I translate this as knowing your strengths, weaknesses, and limitations. This is vital in seeking a loving relationship.

Discovery of the Journey of Love

Dr. Trahern (Tron)

> "Life is a journey and it's about growing and changing and coming to terms with who and what you are and loving who and what you are."
>
> – Kelly McGillis

The journey of discovering love is a lifelong process. I believe love is a journey, not a destination. Love is not what we say; it's what we do. In counseling, I illustrate love as an action that is intentional towards someone else and generates a loving, warm feeling. But when this path is discovered, we must continue to grow and change for the better, as illustrated in the above quote. We can't truly love others unless we love ourselves.

Steps to Discovering True Love

Pastor James

- One, be a real person.
- Two, be kind and tenderhearted as you interact with people.
- Three, emphasize your true self (take off the mask).
- Four, be down to earth or humble.
- Five, be a wise person.

Finding true love is the worthiest pursuit we can engage in. Love is the universal desire of all beings and mammals. In order to find true love, you have to discover what true love is.

Steps to Discovering True Love

Dr. Trahern (Tron)

The step to discovering true love consists of identifying what true love is and taking action towards attaining it.

1. One must discover one's own value and self-worth within oneself.
2. One must take steps towards loving themselves kindly before they can love others. One cannot give what they have not possessed. I have experienced couples in counseling desiring for their partner to change to meet their relational needs. Sadly, it was fruitless. Why did this plea not work? Because change must come from within. Therefore, I aim to have individuals look within to identify steps necessary for change.
3. The next step is respect for oneself and another human being. When you love someone, you respect that person's boundaries.

Love That Lasts

Pastor James

Learn how to extend love impressions to others. This is sort of like sending out love vibrations. The Bible illustrates this concept in the statement, walk in love. We are admonished to behave like Paul noted in Ephesians 5:2 *"And walk in love, as Christ also hath loved us, and hath given himself for us an offering and a sacrifice to God for a sweet-smelling savior."*

This verse encourages us to communicate in a loving way by reaching out to people and connecting with others. In creating love that lasts, we must always speak to the humanity in all people. Listen without judgment and pay attention to other people's feelings.

In my counseling ministry, I notice a pattern of people waiting to react instead of listening to the feelings of others. Here are some strategies to help build lasting love.

First, try to understand what is being said. When we listen to people's feelings and understand what others are saying, it can build loving interactional patterns. Second, speak to people in a joyful expression. Third, we must be positive when others are negative. Four, be good and kind in the way you interact with people. Five, foster positivism by studying positive people.

In order to establish loving and lasting relationships, we must endeavor to develop strong social ties by surrounding ourselves with positivity so we can learn to be positive. Practice mindfulness by focusing more on the present.

As stated in the Serenity Prayer, live one day at a time, enjoying one moment at a time. Be optimistic and always affirm that everything is going to turn out alright. Let's practice what the psalmist did in the prayer, I will rejoice in the Lord at all times (Psalms 34:1).

Love That Lasts

Dr. Trahern (Tron)

> "Love never gives up, never loses faith, is always hopeful, and endures through every circumstance."
>
> Apostle Paul, 1 Corinthians 13:7

We all can agree that we like things that don't give up. For instance, we like our cars to work properly and not break down while driving. We appreciate our phones when they work adequately so we can make calls when needed. We also like for our business or employers not to give way when we need them the most. This means receiving equal pay for a day's work. So, we can all agree we like things to work properly.

What about human relationships? The apostle Paul says there is a love that never fails. Have you ever experienced a love that never fails? We all know the feeling of having something not give up or give in on us. Sadly, nearly 50% of marriages end in broken promises. The promise of love was broken. This is a heart-wrenching feeling. I've seen firsthand individuals who have experienced feelings of brokenness because of a failed relationship. I believe it was never intended to be that way, but there are many forces that work against love lasting forever. Paul gives us three words that are essential for our relationship: faith, hope, and love. In counseling, I use the metaphor of house building to illustrate essential qualities necessary for building a sound and proper relational foundation. These three qualities, if applied consistently, can help love last forever.

How to Love Yourself More Fully

Pastor James

Loving oneself is a life criterion. It is a birthright. What does it mean to love yourself? When we love ourselves, we have an appreciation for our worth and our value. Loving thyself means having trust, pride, and confidence in your God-given abilities. These abilities guide us effectively through life. The need for self-love is an innate need. Human beings must learn to love themselves as soon as they are born. This distinct love is about caring for oneself and looking out for the needs of others.

How does the process begin? First, we must accept ourselves. Self-acceptance begins with a daily practice of mindfulness. Self-acceptance is the ability to accept things we cannot change. It is about noticing resistance that keeps us from loving ourselves more fully. We must focus on taking care of our mental and emotional needs. If we encounter barriers, let us not be afraid to seek mental health counseling. To love oneself, it is important that we continually engage in self-care. We must engage in behaviors that promote good health. According to research, health management involves eating healthy, exercising often, and getting adequate rest. Wellness includes mental, spiritual, and emotional health. We must take care of aspirational needs. We attend to our spiritual needs through group participation in spiritual services.

Additionally, we should engage in daily activities that delight us. These are activities that enhance our feelings about ourselves. When you feel good about yourself, you can achieve more in life. It is God's will that we love ourselves more fully. In Matthew 22: 37-40, it says, *"Jesus said unto him, thou shalt love the Lord thy God with all thy heart, and with all thy soul, and with all thy mind. This is the first and greatest commandment. And the second is like unto it, thou shalt love thy neighbor as thyself."* When we practice this verse, we learn to love ourselves sufficiently. When this happens, we can reach our full potential in life. We become more positive. And we can love others more completely.

How to Love Yourself More Fully

Dr. Trahern (Tron)

We can't give what we don't have. How can one love others when they struggle to love themselves? Many couples have come to my office wanting to be loved more fully. I'm always fascinated to hear love stories. But what do you do when the love given is not reciprocated? The individuals who struggle to reciprocate love sometimes feel trapped in the maze of trying to love themselves more freely. It's challenging to see the ebb and flow of relational dynamics. It is like a roller coaster where one person feels love or struggles to love themselves. When I encounter these individuals, I assess them for confidence and hope. I might ask on a scale of one to ten, one being no confidence and ten being very confident, where are you today in terms of being confident the relationship will work out? Then, I assess hope. I ask where you are today in terms of hopefulness about the relationship. Through assessment, we're able to identify the relational needs and create a treatment plan to mend the feelings of brokenness in their relationship.

Here are some strategies I suggest to help one love more freely.

1. Develop a belief in God and in yourself.
2. Wake up every morning with enthusiasm because negativity can be a drain on relationships.
3. Acknowledge the hurt from the past and how difficult it may be and be willing to move on.
4. Affirm that God loves you, and you love yourself.
5. Replace all negative thoughts daily. Imagine your mind as a beautiful temple.
6. Affirm others through positive and encouraging statements!
7. Become a giver, not a taker.
8. Develop an attitude of gratitude. Daily express three things you're grateful for at the beginning and end of your day.
9. Remove yourself from any individuals who drain your vitality.
10. Affirm daily that you are on the winning team.

Chapter 4

Finding Purpose and Meaning

Pastor James

Do a self-analysis of how you feel about your value. What are your strengths and weaknesses in dealing with life challenges? Search for the pathway that will help you to think and feel differently about the true value and worth about your life.

Discovering purpose and meaning in life is the most important thing that we can do. The big questions are: who am I, what is my reason for being here, and what is my destiny? These are spiritual questions as well as philosophical questions. The Bible states, "I know the plans that I have for you declares the Lord. Plans to prosper you, and not to harm you, plans to give you hope, and a future (Jer 29:11). You can be anything you want to be. Do anything that you set out to accomplish. Having goals and direction in life, be driven to rise every day with determination to put your best foot forward. Make a choice that you are not going to be mediocre. Resolve that you are going to be a difference-maker.

What is the best way to pursue your goals? What will inspire you to get something done in life? Bring others with you. Get somebody to go across the road with you. Find God. He is in your soul. You must make that supreme discovery. Let us explore some ideas to find your purpose.

Learn about your history.
1. Imagine your possibilities.
2. Don't be unwilling to struggle.
3. Allow the shame you feel to push you.
4. Put God first in everything that you do. Get rid of grudges.
5. Be proactive.
6. Be proud of your work.
7. Bring others along.
8. Be passionate about helping the youth.
9. Be ready to heed the call.
10. Recognize that you cannot affect change alone.
11. Desire to make the team.

So, what does it mean to find purpose in life? Finding purpose in life means finding out who we are and learning what we are in the world to do. Every person is born with gifts and talent. What are those talents or gifts? Do talents and gifts give us the ability to make a difference in life?

I have discovered it's challenging trying to discover what we were meant to do. In my own life, it took years to discover my God-given calling. It was like searching for a needle in a haystack. But through divine guidance and support from loved ones, I found the key to unlock my God-given talent. Once I discovered my purpose, I hastened up the path of purpose. What kind of impact are you supposed to make on the world?

Now, take a moment to reflect and look within, and ask yourself what is life's purpose. I have thought long and hard about this. I believe a life of purpose can be defined as discovering who we are at the core.

How does one get to the core? I call it the fire within. It is the thing that motivates us and ignites our passion. What drives you? What are you living for? Let us go on an exploration to find out our purpose.

Dr. Trahern (Tron)

"The two most important days in life are the day you are born and the day you find out why."

– Mark Twain

Everyone has a life purpose. I believe we were all born for something significant. You may be asking: how do I know? I discovered there are billions of people on the planet, and everyone is different. Yes, individuals have similarities in personalities, makeup, and character traits. However, when looking at our design and genetic makeup, we are different. So, how do we discover our purpose? First, it is easy to say, but it takes time, trial, and error to discover. Many times, we chase dreams and goals to later discover it is vanity or they do not give us lasting fulfillment. I believe we should let our passions drive our purpose in life. When we are passionate about a thing, I believe we can achieve it. Where is your passion directed? Sadly, some have allowed insecurity and fear to take the wheel of their lives and drive them into wrong relationships and situations. But the moment we take possession of our lives, we are on the road to discovery.

Finding purpose and meaning in life is essential. It motivates us to jump out of bed in the morning. It is fuel igniting the engine of our lives. Giving us a burning desire to make a difference in the world. But what do we do when our world has been turned upside down? How does one find meaning when a relationship is broken or a cherished loved one dies? What happens when we feel our purpose has been broken to pieces? As a therapist, I believe my job is to help individuals and families live purposeful and meaningful lives.

In the helping profession, I see people at their best and worst moments of life. My aim is to help clients reach their goals. I believe we can reach our goals in life, but it takes faith, determination, and belief in our God-given abilities. This gives us motivation and enthusiasm when we feel discouraged. Perhaps you feel discouraged, and your tank is on E. So, what to do when we face challenges and feel hope fading.

In the toughest times, how do we search for what Viktor Frankl called a search for life's meaning? The first thing to do is look in what I call a manual for living. If we have car trouble, we look in the manual. If we have ailments in our bodies, we get a medical examination to see what our bloodwork reveals. I am recommending turning to the sacred writing of the Bible to discover your purpose. I have found the Bible to be my GPS

(Global Positioning System). When I got all mixed up in the wrong direction, on the wrong streets of life, I went to the manual to get back on track. Have you ever felt lost with nowhere to turn for answers? Even as a licensed professional, I am mindfully aware of the power of faith to solve life's difficulties.

I believe the Bible where Jeremiah sheds light on purpose. One day, I read, "Before I formed thee in the belly, I knew thee; and before thou camest forth out of the womb I sanctified thee, and I ordained thee a prophet unto the nations." These words leaped off the page at me because of their reminder that I was born for a purpose.

How to Discover My Purpose

Pastor James

> *"It is not what we get. But who we become, what we contribute... that gives meaning to our lives."*
>
> **Tony Robbins**

First, you must write down the things that are most important to you in chronological order. Second, do a self-inventory to catch what you are good at. Third, think about how you can use your strengths to add value to the world. Fourth, believe and affirm and say, "I can make a positive difference in the world." These are some of the keys to unlocking your purpose. I believe life presents us with doors of opportunity. The key is unlocking the door to purpose. Then, we will experience joy for living.

How to Live a Purposeful Life

Dr. Trahern (Tron)

A purposeful life is a life that is moving towards an aspiration. William James, a great psychologist, said your hopes, dreams, and aspirations are legitimate. They are trying to take you airborne, above the clouds, above the storms, if you only let them.

I believe we were all born for a purpose. From the time that we are born, we seek to find out what we are created to do and to be in life. This is not an easy task. It takes trial and error. But once it is found, it gives purpose and meaning for living. These goals or aspirations give us a reason to get out of bed in the morning. Recently, I was working with a group of adolescents. We were discussing how we wake up in the morning. They asked me, "Do you wake up with excitement?" As I pondered their question, I realized while I woke up with joy, there was still room to improve my batting average. Meaning I could become more proficient in the enthusiasm I approached each day with. From that time on, I decided to jump out of bed and say, "This is the day the Lord has made. I will rejoice and be glad in it!" With hands lifted in the air, I find this to be a great boost to my day.

Intrinsic Value

Pastor James

It is good to be aware of your intrinsic values. This means getting in touch with your passion. Get clarity on what inspires you. Think about what makes you happy. Be aware of what excites your spiritual joy.

I describe this as being connected to the cosmos. What gives you the feeling of being connected to the universe? I have met with countless individuals who feel disconnected. There are various reasons why these individuals are sitting on the sidelines of life.

Some were not willing to pay the price. I have found the price tag for a life of meaning and purpose is expensive. What price are you willing to pay to discover your gifts and talents? Perhaps we need to learn and grow to best serve our goals. When we gain knowledge, we can clearly identify our best talents and gifts.

Intrinsic Value

Dr. Trahern (Tron)

Life is a beautiful gift that we should value. Should life be valued based on achievements or accomplishments? I believe intrinsic value is our own worth separate from external achievements. Once, I met a man who had a massive amount of wealth. His professional abilities and skills led him to acquire an abundance of external things. But one day, and after much contemplation, he came to discover that he lacked peace. Upon further inquiry, this man would have given anything to experience peace of mind. I have discovered that there are things that we should value for their own sake. Things such as life, health, and strength. Perhaps you have gifts that have intrinsic value. Take a moment and take an inventory of important things in your life, such as loved ones, friends, faith, and core values. Maybe we should focus our attention on things that can't be taken away from us. Considered the story of a father who was teaching his daughter a lesson in intrinsic value.

> "So, I'm explaining intrinsic value to my four-year-old daughter — who loves toy cats — and ask her, if she was really thirsty in the desert, whether she would like a bottle of water, or a toy cat, and she tells me that she would like a bottle of water in the shape of a toy cat."
>
> — Stefan Molyneux

Growing up, I heard the idiom you can't have your cake and eat it too. I found it to be quite confusing because if I had cake, logically, I would want to eat it. However, there was a different meaning, suggesting that there are things that compete for first place in your life. What does it mean you can't have your cake and eat it too? It means that we cannot mutually hold on to competing things. In counseling, when there is a deficit in intimate relationships such as husband and wife, I usually probe to find out what is competing for first place in a person's life that is robbing the other person of the proper place in each other 's lives.

Looking Within

Pastor James

When I counsel individuals, I encourage them to do self-exploration. I call it looking deep within. Then probe and ask honestly: who am I? Why am I here? What is my chief aim in life? In what ways am I gifted? What kind of impact can I make on the world?

Why do I explore these avenues? Because they lead to curiosity about what is most important in life. Sometimes, we can get lost in life. Like the prodigal son in the Bible, we find ourselves in the pigpen of life. When this happens, we need a strength stronger than ourselves to get out.

Getting unstuck requires prayer to ask God to reveal the purpose of life.

Looking Within

Dr. Trahern (Tron)

Have you ever had a closet or storage that was left so long that you were afraid to open it and look at it? Many times, the rooms in our lives can be so cluttered with things such as unforgiveness, past resentments, and hurts it's fearful to look at. When this happens, it requires professional help or a competent spiritual advisor to overcome the emotional pain. This is no easy process because it is fearful to look within at areas of defect in our character that we need to work on.

Here are three suggestions to begin the process. First, we should self-examine and see how we feel about some people in past circumstances. Once we identify these feelings, perhaps we should seek help with these maladies. Second, we should pray and ask for divine guidance on how to remedy these ills of the past. Finally, we should let go of the past and move forward. This step will not be easy because sometimes we are accustomed to looking in the rearview mirror of life. When we are tempted to do this, let us remember that the windshield of our future is larger than the rearview mirror of the past.

Your Action Steps

Pastor James

Seek your purpose until you find it. Your purpose is the thing that you are most passionate about. It is this core value that you are living for. So, what are you going to do about this?

Before you get too far down the road of life, stop and count the cost of putting your purpose into action. Be willing to pay the price of actualizing your purpose. Meet the challenge by hard work.

Your Action Steps

Dr. Trahern (Tron)

To have purposeful relationships, everyone must be intentional about fulfilling their mutual roles. For example, on a well-functioning basketball team, there are point guards and forwards in the centers. For the team to achieve success, each player must adhere to their assigned roles. In these functional families, everyone fights for the ball. Everyone wants to take the shot. Imagine if you were watching a basketball game, and during the game, a person snatches the ball out of a teammate's hand and takes the shot. You would be shocked to see this type of transaction. Sadly, this happens too often in families. I've seen couples selfishly snatching the ball out of their spouse's hand because they wanted to take the shot. Perhaps they wanted to spend money or go shopping during a time when

Finding Purpose and Meaning

finances were needed for something else. Or maybe they want it their way and then motion to cut off and block the harmony in their relationship. Maybe they got on the phone and called a friend to spill over all of their relational problems.

On the other hand, siblings also fight for the ball. Instead of playing fairly, if they can't have all the shots, they take their balls and go home. This is illustrated by wanting all the praise from parents and crowding out their siblings. This creates tension and unresolved conflicts. So, how do we make purposeful relationships happen? There must be teamwork. There must be a goal for relationships. There must be fairness, and they will miss working together. There must be unity. There must be unselfishness. There must be willingness to forgive others.

Chapter 5

Discovering a Path to Personal Enrichment

How to Live a Personal Enriched Life

Pastor James

Live by faith; live by trust in the power that is greater than everyone else. "Live under the shadow of the Almighty. Look at life with the perspective that life is not about you. It is about the others in your life, it is about your family, your friends, and who else God puts in your life." Let us look for a personal enriched life. And let us not stop until we find it. It is said that a person needs just three things in this world to be happy: someone to love, something to do, and something to hope for. (Country Living.com)

The Bible says that the three greatest gifts in life are charity, faith, and hope. Charity is the greatest.1 Corinthians 13: Enter on the path that leads to personal enrichment by praying to God, asking for courage, strength, and wisdom.

To find the path to achievement, we must ask ourselves: what do I want to achieve in life? We must do self-examination. As we reflect on our strengths and weaknesses, we should seek divine help. Ask God for direction. We should be determined to be the best version of ourselves we can be. This happens through seeking help and studying principles of success. We must apply principles of success to build a successful life. We must believe in ourselves. Pray for wisdom and divine guidance. We must use setbacks as motivation to work harder and wiser. We must associate with people who can provide positive affirmations for us. We must engage in positive self-talk and use prayers to cast negativity out of our minds. One intervention that is important is the Serenity Prayer. We should pray this prayer many times every day. We should put forth our best effort through hard work every day. We should work to love ourselves more fully. We must love ourselves before we can love others.

How to Live a Personal Enriched Life

Dr. Trahern (Tron)

Merriam-Webster defined self-entrenchment as the act or process of increasing one's intellectual or spiritual resources.

"Son, if you know God and you are educated, no one can look down on you." These words rang from the lips of my father. At the time, I did not grasp its meaning. Did he repeat these words often because his father had a third-grade education? The reason he stopped at grade three was to care for his mother and sister after the sudden death of his father. Perhaps my father grappled with the fact his father, who was a strong man of faith, had to teach himself how to read, or was it the stress of rearing five children and having to return to night school as an adult? Maybe this was the driving force behind my father's stressing what he believed was necessary for a well-adjusted life. Faith in God, education, and hard work. While there are others, these three were the overarching themes at our kitchen table.

Perhaps there was one more factor that fueled my father and mother's passion for us to excel. It was the history of the struggle. In some way, I believe all these factors were interwoven.

How does personal enrichment happen? I believe it occurs when an individual gets a burning desire to utilize their talents and abilities to reach their full potential in life. It is never too late to pursue a dream or a goal. But one must be willing to take the first step.

"You don't have to see the whole staircase; just take the first step."

Martin Luther King Jr.

Perhaps you have been waiting for the right time to begin your journey of personal enrichment. We can't wait till we feel motivated to act. We must act even if we don't feel like it. I learned in professional sports that you must play even when you don't feel like playing. Because to be successful, you're going to have to go against the current. This means you're going to have to fight feelings. Emotional baggage can be a roadblock to personal and spiritual enrichment. Take a moment to visualize yourself reaching your goals. How will you feel when you have reached the plateau of spiritual and personal enrichment?

Would you like to live a life that's more enriching emotionally, mentally, financially, relationally, and spiritually? It's possible, but we must develop an action plan. Consider our action plan that one man discovered. When his colleague asked what it is that kept him vital, he responded that he woke up daily and began his day with meditation in time with his Creator.

How to Pursue a Life of Personal Achievement: Let Us Strive to Think Biblically. It Will Profit Us Greatly.

Pastor James

A personal and enriched life is a life that is inspired by joy and filled with happiness. It is a life that is fueled by inner peace. I believe true peace is an inner quality. This inner peace can be acquired through prayer, meditation, and studying the Bible. These are positive spiritual exercises to help enrich our lives. So, how can we cultivate a more personal, enriching life? Here are twelve positive things that we can practice or engage in daily to build an enriching life. One, practice gratitude. Practicing gratitude by extenuating the positive and noticing the good things around you. We should cultivate a habit of giving thanks always. Two, we must believe that we can have self-control. This happens when the spirit of God is active in our lives. Three, we must recognize the need for growth. Four, we must change negative thoughts. Five, change your story. Six, get rid of negative thought patterns and systems. Seven, face your fears. Eight, focus on success, not failure. Nine, see problems as gifts. Ten, appreciate yourself. Eleven, engage in social stimulation through engaging with others. Twelve, we must engage in spiritual nourishment. Like the physical body requires physical food and water, spiritually, we must develop an appetite for the word of God.

How to Pursue a Life of Personal Achievement: Let Us Strive to Think Biblically. It Will Profit Us Greatly.

Dr. Trahern (Tron)

To begin the journey of personal enrichment, one must have a goal in mind. For instance, no one sets out to run a marathon without taking the proper steps. One must have proper gear and training. Likewise, in the journey of life, one must have the proper spiritual, emotional, mental, and relational enrichment to reach love heights. I don't believe anyone can achieve a worthy goal without the support of others. Growing up, I always used to hear the statement, "It takes a village." Sometimes, I hear people saying it takes "me" or "I" to succeed.

Here are ten strategies to help you begin the process of personal and spiritual enrichment.

1. Identify what it is that you want out of life.
2. Find a mentor or advisor who is doing what you desire to do.
3. Make up your mind that you're going to pursue your dream.
4. Work towards your goal despite how you feel.
5. Develop a habit of meditation and prayer, which is a tonic against discouragement.
6. Do not share your dreams or goals with dream killers.
7. Limit time on social media and TV; that time could be reallocated towards something more productive.
8. No matter how hard it gets, don't quit.

9. Attend to your physical, mental, and emotional well-being.
10. After reaching your goal, go back and help mentor someone else to achieve their goals.

Statistics on People Who Are Enriched

Pastor James

What are the statistics on living a personally enriched life? According to research, there are five areas of life that contribute to well-being or enrichment: "happiness and life satisfaction, physical and mental health, meaning and purpose, character and virtue, and close social relationships" (Lee, *Pursuing Happiness and Health,* 2020).

These individuals' happiness was not based on the amount of money they possessed. They were living a meaningful, purposeful life. So, how does one live an enriched life? In essence, enrichment is moving forward towards goals. It's a life that overcomes challenges. It's a life of joy and satisfaction.

How does one discover this meaningful, enriched life? First, one must discover true wealth is far more than monetary gain. There was a Harvard study of seventy-five individuals over their lifetime (Liz Mineo, "Harvard Study, Almost 80 Years Old, Has Proved That Embracing Community Helps Us Live Longer, and Be Happier," 2017). The study found that close relationships, more than money or fame, make people happy throughout their lives.

Close relational ties produce satisfaction in life. The Harvard study establishes a strong correlation between deep relationships and well-being. Unfortunately, many fall short of living a truly fulfilled life.

Statistics on People Who Are Enriched

Dr. Trahern (Tron)

Have you ever spent time with a person who uplifted your mood? In reflection, your time with this person was so satisfying. Too often, we experience the opposite. If the truth is told, we all know people who can deplete us. They zap our energy and leave us feeling down in the dumps. But the enriched person is like jumper cables. They can boost your system. If you are feeling broken down, they can help lift you up. Question: In the last month, how many people have you encountered that made your nervous system feel good?

According to IPSOS, a world survey was conducted. Its findings suggested that across the world, people must look to their health and well-being (both physical and mental), their family (partner/spouse and children), and having a sense of purpose as what gives them "the greatest happiness." Next comes their living conditions, feeling safe and in control, being in nature, having a meaningful job, and having more money (Skinner, What makes people happiest? Health, family, and purpose, 2022).

Engagement in Purposeful Habits

Pastor James

Engaging in purposeful habits is a daily practice. I have discovered the practice of spiritual enrichment improves every aspect of the practitioner's life. Countless studies have shown living a spiritual life dramatically increases the total well-being and wealth of a person's life.

Here are some strategies on how to live a meaningful life. First, be mindful of your thoughts. Two, do things to dramatically enrich your life now. Three, seek out principles on how to cultivate a more rewarding lifestyle. Four, live in the present moment without judging yourself or others. Five, focus on the present and on the beauty around us. Six, practice being still. Seven, seek wisdom on how to accomplish your goals through prayers and meditation.

Engagement in Purposeful Habits

Dr. Trahern (Tron)

> "Excellence is an art won by training and habituation."
>
> – Aristotle

If we want to achieve success in life, we must cultivate winning habits. As a former professional athlete, I have learned the value of developing good work habits. Every championship team I played on possessed disciplines and habits of hard work, determination, commitment, and preparation.

As we begin the journey of engaging in purposeful habits, let us examine our current habits. How are our eating habits? My NFL team used to say your body is your business. This means that to perform at the optimal level, self-care must be prioritized. How is overall wellness of mind, body, and spirit? Do you have good rest habits, relational habits, and spiritual habits? I believe purposeful habits are a lifestyle. It is something we must engage in repeatedly, day in and day out, even when we do not feel like it.

When I became serious about pursuing my goal of making it to the NFL, I cultivated winning habits. I decided to do the little things some players were not willing to do. For example, after a long, grueling practice, I would stay after practice and work on my technique to strengthen my skill and ability. Perhaps you are a step away from a dream, but you must go the extra mile. While the extra mile looks different for each person, it is necessary if you want to be above average.

For me, staying extra when I did not feel like it was going the extra mile. Maybe you should put in an additional hour of study or stay a little later at the job to complete the task or work on a relationship that's in need of repair.

"If you want something you've never had, you must be willing to do something you've never done."

— Thomas Jefferson

If you want to go where you have never gone before, you must do something you have never done before.

How to Engage in Purposeful Habits

Pastor James

Decide that you want to get rid of every habit that besets you. Talk to friends about the habit that you want to break. Ask for support from your friends. Do research on how to change bad habits. Prepare yourself for the challenge of the change that you want to make. Pray about it and get started.

We must resolve to cultivate good habits. This happens when we are inspired to move forward towards a desired dream or goal. Having goals is vital for success in one's life. We must decide what we want to do in life. Who do you want to be? Finally, we must do crucial inventory to discover what is necessary for goal achievement. I have discovered a price must be paid to achieve success in life. Determine what price you are willing to pay for the achievement of your purpose in life.

First, set your intentions and focus on your desires. For instance, as an archer sets a target, we must set our aim on the goal. After counting the costs and setting the goals, we must invest time and effort in pursuing our goals.

Here are some action steps for the attainment of goals. Start with a plan and be persistent. We must aim for a vision in our minds. Next, create a personal vision statement. Write the key statement about your value. Write a clear plan on how you expect to achieve your intended purpose. Gather data in other fields of your pursuit. We must continue to ask questions. Work hard and stay focused on your dreams. Be mindful of your thoughts. Seek out principles on how to cultivate a more rewarding lifestyle. Five steps for breaking bad habits.

1. Start one-to-one conversations with each family member.
2. Substitute bad habits for good ones.
3. Make small changes at a time.
4. Pay attention to why you engage in the bad habit.
5. Make a clear plan on how to quit.

How to Engage in Purposeful Habits

Dr Trahern (Tron)

First, we must start from where we are. We must do some serious thinking about our goals. What is that thing that I truly desire? Perhaps it is a better relationship, better marriage, to be a better parent, have better health, better financial security, a better spiritual life, or better personal development. The key is to start immediately.

Many times, we have goals, but we're waiting to act. It is like a person stuck on an island. He might have the resources at his disposal to get off the island, but if he does not act, he will remain stuck. Perhaps you feel stuck in habits that are not serving you well. To engage in purposeful habits, we must take inventory of our lives and see what is lacking. Just the other day, I was in the grocery store, and I saw an electronic device taking inventory of what was missing in each aisle. I was fascinated to see such a contraption. If systems are created to inventory products, we would do well to examine our lives for what is missing. It is not easy to be mindfully aware of what is missing. Perhaps the missing ingredients are what is missing to help us achieve our purpose.

Take a moment to reflect on your goals and desires. What action steps must you take to be the best you can be? This means we take steps towards a goal and work towards it every day, no matter how we feel. When you begin to act towards your goals, you will feel a sense of enrichment. It goes without saying that being true and rich means we're constantly improving and getting better and better every day.

How to Enrich the Family

Pastor James

"Rejoice with your family in the beautiful land of life."
Albert Einstein

Family is a network of people connected by bloodline, values, traditions, and mostly by faith. The family is necessary. It is the foundation of progeny. We must always reach out to the family unit in love. Family enrichment is the acquisition of knowledge and skills that strengthen the family system, which creates more positive bonds. It is a search for resources and services for improving the family.

Firstly, each family member needs to seek out ways of understanding their own emotions, such as anxiety, fear, guilt, and anger. When family members experience high levels of social anxiety, this may cause them to look at the world in negative ways. They may feel that everyone is wrong and against them. Such feelings and thoughts hinder them from developing and maintaining closeness inside their relationships. When a member or members experience these kinds of abnormalities, it can result in long-term anger and mistrust.

Secondly, families need to connect by reaching out to each other in helpful ways. Communicating with family and doing nice things for them helps to build strong relationships. This step requires doing and saying kind things to each other. Also, one must do their part in carrying weight and bearing the load at the time. As we communicate and interact with the goal of enriching our family members, we take the positive path.

Thirdly, handle all conflict carefully and sensitively. Make it your goal to foster a sense of community and teamwork. Identify the strength of each family member. Use their strengths to continue to enhance the quality of the group.

Lastly, we must mitigate positive outcomes by working with family strengths. The leaders of the families are chosen for this task. This person seeks to ease the tension in family relations through having one-on-one meetings with the individuals in the group.

The action sets are to call family members and to create a comfortable space where all members can express their concerns and differences. One must be a good listener with great empathy.

How to Enrich the Family

Dr. Trahern (Tron)

What is an enriching family? An enriched family is one where all its members feel valued and appreciated. Early on, we discussed Felicity and Tiffany. These sisters were raised in a family of four. Although their parents were highly successful in their careers, they lacked the ingredients to create a harmonized home where its members were treated as equals.

Creating equality in human relationships is not easy. It takes awareness and intentionality for relational fairness to happen. To illustrate, I will use a banking example. In the case example, it was evident that Felicity received more relational deposits than Tiffany. When unfairness happens in any relationship, it creates disharmony. Sadly, over time, it deteriorates the relationship. Perhaps parents, caregivers, and loved ones are unaware of these mishaps. It intentionally happens when one takes action to break negative patterns that cause relationships to get stuck

I believe the first step in creating an enriched family is to show appreciation for each person in the family system. I believe appreciation is like water to a garden. When gardens receive proper nourishment, they grow; likewise, when individuals receive words of affirmation and encouragement, they grow. Additionally, it makes the person feel good on the inside. Have you ever talked with someone who gave you a warm glow inside as they communicated with you? What was it about that interaction that created this warmth? Was it the tone of their voice? Was it the smile on their face? Was it the care that they showed? While it can be difficult to measure, we know how it makes us feel. Perhaps many individuals and families are starving for a word of appreciation or encouragement. Maybe a word of encouragement will help that struggling child feel more hopeful about their possibilities. Perhaps an act of appreciation will help that wife feel hopeful about her relationship. According to research, everyone desires to be appreciated. Gratitude releases oxytocin, which is a love hormone that in turn builds greater connection and bonds between two individuals. (USU Extension Services)

Action steps to enrich family life

1. Make all members feel appreciated and valued.
2. Celebrate differences.
3. Lift others up with your words.
4. Don't go to bed with pent-up anger.
5. Let go of grievances. Life is too precious to hold on to stuff.
6. Spend quality time together.
7. Disconnect from social media during family time to be fully present.

How to Enrich Your Career

Pastor James

A career is a list of an individual's work history over a considerable amount of time. The career is engaged in as an opportunity for earning a livelihood. When a person feels unfulfilled or uninspired in their course of work, it may lead them to seek to enrich their career opportunity. This will require some in-depth attention.

First, one must begin the process of vocational enrichment by setting a goal. Start searching for a database. Perhaps the best way to begin the career enrichment growth process is to reach out to a career coach. Second, if you are a person of faith, reach out to God or your Higher Power and ask for clarity about how to find one's purpose in life. Third, get a competent assessment of your aptitude for the kind of vocation that you may be best suited for. Ask yourself what kind of work I am best suited for right now. Is it work that I am enthusiastic or excited about? Fourth, do a competency test to match interests, personality traits, and general knowledge for performing a particular job.

Maximize the desire to be more than average in any career that you may be considering. Create a resume that speaks to your strength and professionalism.

See a skilled counselor. Search for skill development opportunities. Determine what price you are willing to pay in hard work, diligence, and determination.

Enriching any aspect of your personal life will take effort and sacrifice to improve your career opportunities. Pursue a better education. Continue to develop computer and technological skills. Extend your network contact with other professionals in your field. Attend seminars and workshops. Talk to people at social functions or religious services. Now, consider four practical points to help you begin moving forward in your career enrichment pursuits.

1. Be willing to finance the cost to advance your education.
2. Stay abreast of growth opportunities in your profession.
3. Be prepared to work from home.
4. Be willing to do more tasks than required.

Is there a career that would cause us to jump out of bed with excitement? It is possible to discover that pathway. An enriched career is one that gives a person a burning passion. It's an inner passion that radiates in all aspects of their work.

How to Enrich Your Career

Dr. Trahern (Tron)

"Find a job you enjoy doing, and you will never have to work a day in your life."

— Mark Twain

Is it possible to wake up every day with enthusiasm about work? Some would argue that is impossible. But according to Mark Twain, if you find enjoyment in your job, you will never work a day in your life. In this section, let's unpack this idea of career satisfaction. Let's begin by doing some self-reflection. How do you feel about your chosen employment status? Do you enjoy your work, or do you dread getting out of bed in the morning? As a matter of fact, why do you go to work? Is it to pay bills, get out of debt, or pay off your student loans? If we were to ask ten people if they really enjoyed their job, how many would say in the affirmative, "Yes, I love what I do!" Let me ask you, do you love what you do? Was there a time when you had more zeal for your job?

Perhaps, like me, you began your career in the job you love, but you were abruptly let go. My first job was a job I always dreamed of doing since my adolescence. My goal was to be a professional athlete. I achieved that goal, and it brought much fulfillment because I was able to realize a goal. But shortly after the achievement of that dream, I was released. I had to start all over again. However, the same passion that led me to the NFL helped me to achieve other goals. I believe many are unhappy in their careers because their passions are buried beneath feelings of hurt, rejection, and disappointment. Perhaps we need to recreate our narrative. To experience career enrichment, we must identify narratives of success. We should conjure up in our thoughts the emotions that led us to pursue our chosen career. I am forty-four years old. Currently, I am working at my second job. In my first career job, I used to jump out of bed, enthusiastic to go to work. The question was whether I could still jump out of bed for my second career with the same zeal and passion that I did during my first career job. At first, it was a challenge. Because fifteen or more years of my life had been dedicated to football. Now, I was faced with the reality of a new normal.

It has been nearly twenty years since I suited up for an NFL team. Currently, I work with abused and neglected children, supervising an evidence-based therapy program to help youth and families experiencing severe behavioral challenges. The same enthusiasm that motivated me to get out of bed for professional sports still accompanies me to work every day.

To illustrate, our motivation and passion for work can be likened to the engine of a car. When we are properly calibrated and tuned up, we can go the distance. Can you still go the distance? Or do you need a tune-up? Maybe a tune-up is changing your thoughts and feelings about your job. Instead of looking at what you don't like, identify what you do like about your job. Begin to set goals and work on new interests. Ask your boss how your talents can best serve the organization.

To have an enriching career, you must begin with a career goal. Ask some probing questions. What is meaningful work? What contribution can I make to the world? This requires some analysis or coaching. Some people are fortunate. They would contend that from the time of adolescence, they knew what they wanted to be in life. Maybe you were reared in a family system that encouraged you to take the path of medical school or dental school or to become a social worker. If these seeds were planted at an early age, you are fortunate. On the other hand, if you had to figure it out through trial and error, you are also fortunate because you know how to solve problems.

My story is about rebuilding and repairing when a dream is lost. If I can make it from the inner city to the NFL, get released, and start all over again, you can do it too.

Here are some action steps to help you in your pursuit of career enrichment.

1. Identify career options that would give you a sense of fulfillment.
2. Set realistic goals.
3. Seek training or career counsel.
4. Find a place to volunteer. Give back.
5. Don't be afraid to start small.
6. Be open-minded and willing to accept criticism.
7. Be a team player.
8. Create a developmental plan and review it often.
9. Cultivate a positive attitude.
10. Jump out of bed every day with excitement, saying this is going to be a great day.

Finally, to sustain career enrichment, always seek to grow and advance professionally.

Advancement is not about the money; it is about maximizing opportunity. My father used to tell me,

"Son, don't worry about the money. If you go out and do a great job, money will take care of itself." When I first heard his words, I did not jump with enthusiasm. On the contrary, I was quite confused because I thought we should ask for what we needed. I remember reading a story in the Bible about the vineyard workers. One of the workers went out late to work, but he was compensated well. While the text does not say this, I believe in one hour, he worked so well with a positive attitude, and he was paid well. Perhaps you should try this technique. For the next fourteen days, get up every day with enthusiasm. Go to work with a servant mindset. Do not complain or murmur. Do not gossip at the water cooler. Be a team player. This will elevate your mood, and your boss will notice the shift. Perhaps the only thing that stands between you and success is your attitude. Wayne Dyer has said that when we change the way we look at things, the things we look at will change. So, take a sheet of paper and write down all the things you like about your job.

Perhaps you're struggling to find things you like about the job. Maybe you should begin with the benefit of having a job because many people are unemployed.

Perhaps you can highlight the flexibility to support your children. Whatever it is, start there. These action steps are important because every job has positives and negatives. But if we can begin to focus on the positive, we will achieve better results.

How to Enrich Students' Lives

Pastor James

Enriching students' lives begins with compassionate and passionate teachers. The teacher needs to be knowledgeable in their field or subject matter. An effective teacher needs to be interesting, caring, and enthusiastic. A good teacher also needs to be well-prepared and zealous. So, what does enriching lives mean?

The enrichment of students' lives is the activity of providing skills and strategies for the growth and development of the student.

Enhancing the student's ability to grow and learn to use knowledge for their betterment. Student enrichment looks for means of offering cognitive and social support for the development of the students' skills. Facilitators come up with programs, activities, and crafts to educate and motivate students to learn.

Working together as a faith and learning community can greatly serve to enhance the lives of students. When parents, grandparents, teachers, clergy, and the village work together on behalf of the students, all benefit. What are some strategies and tips we can use to improve the quality of the lives of the pupils?

1. Help students develop faith, confidence, and self-motivation.
2. Enhance students' desires, passions, and feelings for personal growth. Help students

to determine their goals. Expose students to a well-thought-out growth program. Encourage students to practice.
3. Mentoring and tutoring help students turn bad grades around and instill confidence. Encourage students to get one-on-one tutoring.
4. Teach students to use a step-by-step method for solving problems. Focus on connecting with students. Create a positive and supportive learning atmosphere.
5. Use questions and ask for feedback. Asking questions and for feedback clarifies their thinking and provides understanding.
6. Create a collaborative community to inform and inspire and so that students feel confident about themselves. When students feel confident, they are more likely to be emotionally strong and successful learners.

Enriched Students

Dr. Trahern (Tron)

> "Strive to make something of yourself, then strive to make the most of yourself."
>
> —Michelle Obama

Enriching students means striving to enhance the quality of academic achievement. Student enrichment is a systemic endeavor. It takes a village to help a child succeed. I believe academic excellence extends beyond the classroom into the home and community. Community is a faith-based organization that addresses the holistic needs of a child. Currently, I facilitate a youth empowerment group at my local church. On a weekly basis, we seek to inspire adolescents to maximize opportunities. The aim of the class is to inspire youth to prosper spiritually, emotionally, mentally, socially, and academically. In the First Lady Obama quote, she encouraged individuals to strive to make the most of themselves. I translate this to mean, give life 100% effort. Recently, I asked our youth group to list all their classes and the names of their teachers. Then, I asked them to give me an effort percentage for each class. While some of the youth gave 100% daily effort, some did not give it their all.

In life, each student is given an opportunity, but one must be prepared to take advantage of the God-given gifts given. This means to be prepared to walk through doors of opportunity.

Dr. King said, "If a man is called to be a street sweeper, he should sweep streets even as Michelangelo painted, Beethoven composed music, or Shakespeare wrote poetry. He should sweep streets so well that all the hosts of heaven and Earth will pause to say, here lived a great street sweeper who did his job well." In the scriptures, the apostle Paul told young Timothy, "Throw yourself into your tasks so that everyone will see your progress." In order to be an enriched student, one must give maximum effort daily. They are not shortcuts to success. So, when should this process of student enrichment begin?

Student enrichment should start as early as possible. What if all parents started enrichment from the time their child learned to walk? According to Erickson's early stage of development, parents should begin the process of instilling values of educational enrichment early. Perhaps they are beginning to read to their child and teach phonetics. I believe education is a lifelong pursuit.

How to Enrich Students' Lives

> "First comes thought; then organization of that thought into ideas and plans; then transformation of those plans into reality."
>
> — Napoleon Hill, The Law of Success

In this section, I will provide five strategies to help students have an enhanced life. The first step is to become organized. Organization is the first step in students advancing academically. To illustrate, it is hard to focus in a cluttered house. Have you ever had a cluttered house or bedroom? Perhaps it blocked creativity from flowing. When stuff is everywhere, it is hard to focus. Likewise, when our minds are cluttered, we don't know where to start. Napoleon Hill suggested that there is a correlation between our thoughts and organization. The first step is to have clear thoughts, which leads to organization. For students to begin the process of enrichment, it must start with organized thoughts and goals.

Step two is to be disciplined. To be successful, one must practice self-discipline. I define self-discipline as doing something when you don't feel like it or one's ability to delay gratification while they are working towards a goal.

Step three is hard work. There is no substitution for hard work. For a student to excel, they have to be willing to put in the work.

Step four is overall health and wellness. To be your best, one must be well physically, mentally, and emotionally. This means a proper diet, proper rest, and a clear mind.

Finally, step five is having a mentor or advisor. Mentorship is a tonic in dealing with the challenges and rigors of academic success.

The Enrichment of Friendships

Pastor James

Developing and encouraging lasting friendships is a lifelong process. A key aspect of a healthy friendship is letting friends know that you care about and appreciate them. If we want to enrich our friendships, we can begin by increasing our communication. Here are some practical steps for improving friendships.

1. We must focus on the positive.
2. Show appreciation.
3. Get to know each other.
4. Accent the attribute of your friend.

The Enrichment of Friendships

Dr. Trahern (Tron)

> "A friend is one that knows you as you are, understands where you have been, accepts what you have become, and still gently allows you to grow."
>
> – William Shakespeare

The enrichment of friendships is vital to life. When I was growing up, my father used to say, "Son, if you can find one or two good friends in life, you have done well." This statement has served me well because it gave me an appreciation of the friends who have invested in my life. True friends look out for your overall well-being, and they tell you the truth even when you don't want to hear it. Enriched friends are individuals you can turn to during challenging times to give you a word of encouragement. How do we develop authentic friendships?

1. One must be a friend to develop friendships.
2. Show care and concern for others.
3. Be open to growth and appreciate the perspectives of others.
4. Be a kind person.

Enriched Spiritual Life

Pastor James

"This I say then, Walk in the Spirit, and ye shall not fulfil the lust of the flesh.

Galatians 5:16 KJV

The life enriched by the spirit brings more fulfillment to life. Living a spiritual life influences many of the decisions that people make in a positive way. The practice of spiritual enrichment helps to build greater self-esteem and confidence. This practice will also promote overall wholeness and betterment. Spiritual enrichment offers the pathway for spiritual growth. Every person should desire to grow spiritually. This should be life's chief aim. What is a spiritual life?

The spiritual life is a life rooted in the belief in the idea that we are created and connected to the Ultimate Supreme Being, which is God. He is the life-giving source that has authority over all things. He is the gift that replenishes. We need a vital connection with the divine enhancer. How can we participate in the activity of spiritual enriching actions that enhance our well-being?

First, enrichment for our lives requires organizing a plan. Here are some steps we can take to put our plan into action. An effective way to begin the journey of spiritual enrichment is through prayer, meditation, and self-reflection.

Do a personal inventory assessment of your personal strengths. Pray to God and ask for power to build on your strong qualities.

Ask for knowledge and understanding on how to identify the weak areas in your life. Have the courage to admit character defects in your life. First, identify areas to change. Now draw up a well-researched plan for targeting the weak items in your life. Consider why spiritual maturity is important. Think about the reason that you want to grow spiritually.

How to begin the plan of spiritual enrichment? First, pray for insight and strength to unpack the emotional weights from your life. The Bible states if any man lacks wisdom, let him ask of God (James 1:5).

Now let us look at an application verse, Philippians 4:6-7. The principle of spiritual enrichment is to learn to focus our minds and control our thoughts. We must learn to have better control over our emotions by practicing the concepts of the ancient wisdom of the Bible. Secondly, find an accountability partner to hold you responsible for your commitment to change. Then, get to work on your plan. Here are some action steps:

1. Connection: seek to connect to your Higher Power.
2. Practice an awareness of your spiritual needs.
3. Ponder things that matter most.
4. Engage in consistent prevailing prayer.
5. Practice the attitude of gratitude.

6. Practice the discipline of forgiveness.
7. Practice love.
8. Practice scripture memorization.
9. Practice fasting.
10. Practice solitude.

Enriched Spiritual Life

Dr. Trahern (Tron)

What is an enriched spiritual life? An enriched spiritual life is a life of inner peace and satisfaction that comes from a divine connection to the Creator God. And the rich life is also a life that is purposeful and meaningful. To pursue a rich life, one must become detached from things that are material and become connected to the immaterial. About twenty years ago, I was conversing with a professional athlete who had amassed great will. During a conversation about life and purpose, he expressed that he desired peace. The material things of life, such as a fancy car and elaborate home, and the luxuries of life did not meet his deeper needs. John, whose name was changed for the purpose of confidentiality, had discovered that he had deeper needs that only a connection to God would fulfill. After our conversation, he realized the most meaningful and important things in life can't be purchased on the car lot or in department stores. They don't come from elaborate homes or multiple uncommitted relationships.

Consider this quote:

> "Happiness cannot be traveled to, owned, earned, worn, or consumed. Happiness is the spiritual experience of living every minute with love, grace, and gratitude."
>
> – Denis Waitley

Here are some action steps to enrich your life spiritually.

1. Be grateful for life.
2. Give thanks every day for the blessings that you have received.
3. Show compassion for others.
4. Appreciate the beauty of nature.
5. Meditate daily!
6. Pray often.
7. Don't worry about things that you have no control over.
8. Learn to love your neighbor.
9. Practice forgiveness and letting go of grudges.
10. Learn to live within your means and don't compare yourself to others (Mindbodygreen.com).

Chapter 6

Developing Habits that Serve You

How Can Bad Habits Be Defined?

Pastor James

A bad habit can be defined as a pattern of negative behavior.

Destructive or bad habits are any behaviors that cause harm to you or others around you. People continue to engage in bad habits because they receive satisfaction or a psychological boost. But bad habits can be broken and rooted out.

When you are not doing these things, your mind may create a strong, addictive craving for them. People engage in unhealthy habits because they have become socially accepted. The process of changing bad habits takes time to break because the mind is not usually conducive to change. In a sense, the brain works against us. The brain can become hard-wired against the change needed. Another thing that makes habits especially hard to break is that replacing the learned habit with a new one does not remove the original one.

It is difficult to understand why individuals adopt unhealthy habits. It is paradoxical because it does not make sense to continue to do things over and over that cause one trouble.

How Are Habits Defined?

Dr. Trahern (Tron)

According to Wikipedia, "A habit is a routine of behavior that is repeated regularly and tends to occur subconsciously." The *American Journal of Psychology* defined a habit as "a more or less fixed way of thinking, willing, or feeling acquired through previous repetition of a mental experience." Without insight and acknowledgment, habits are impossible to break.

How do we cultivate inspiring habits? Habits that inspire and motivate us to achieve in life? A habit is like fuel to the engine of our lives. To illustrate, if a vehicle has no fuel, it will not go far. I believe good habits help ignite our possibilities. This gives fuel to the engine of our lives.

How do we form good habits? Forming good habits is essential to the pursuit of our goals. Here are action steps to help us form good habits. Firstly, we must set a short- or long-term goal. Secondly, write down the steps it will take to achieve the goal. Thirdly, develop a routine and stick to it daily. Finally, we must identify roadblocks.

When I was on the road to pursuing a professional football career, habits were critical in achieving my goal. I wrote down my goals. I applied action steps. I develop habits of extra training. Finally, I made sacrifices and neglected decisions that would lead to setbacks.

When we neglect good habits, we can fall short of reaching our full potential. Earlier, we illustrated how purpose happens in our lives when we search for it as one would search for gold. Are there habits we need to break? What is the one thing you need to do that would make a difference in your life? What sacrifice are you willing to make to achieve it?

How to Engage in Purposeful Habits

Pastor James

The habit of practicing good goals leads to the cultivation of a much more satisfying life. It is rewarding to live a life guided by your values and spiritual intentions. Therefore, one should endeavor to find their true potential. It is good to resolve to practice the determination to cultivate good habits. Become inspired to move forward towards a desired goal.

Decide what you want to do in life. Who do you want to be? Do a crucial self-inventory. Determine what price you are willing to pay for the achievement of your purpose.

First, set your intention and focus on your aim. Target the goal. After you have counted the cost of what will be needed in time, effort, and sacrifice, now, begin the journey.

Start with a plan of persistence. Visualize a picture of the realization of your personal vision in your mind. Next, create a personal vision statement. Write a key statement about your values concerning your values about the vision. Write a clear plan of how you expect to arrive at the intended purpose. Gather data in other fields of your pursuit. Ask questions. Work hard and stay focused on your dream.

Once we target our valued goal, search for tested principles for reaching goals. It has been said over and over that the number one thing to do to develop a good habit is to practice, practice. Be repetitious in striving toward your goal. Give it all that you have. Go after that goal with reckless abandonment. Have a positive attitude and believe that your goals are possible and within reach.

Things that we can do to reach our goal.

How to chart a course of action for developing positive habits.

1. Sit quietly for five minutes. Think and focus on something spiritual.
2. Pray for power to change negative habits.
3. Participate in thirty minutes of moderate daily exercise.
4. Eat something healthy for breakfast.
5. Drink water.
6. Think about things you have rather than things that you don't have.
7. Monitor your thoughts. Replace negative thoughts with positive thoughts.
8. Read five Bible verses from the Book of Proverbs daily.
9. Read a chapter from a personal development book daily.
10. Don't take everything personally.
11. Cherish the moment.
12. Perfect an attitude of gratitude.
13. Just smile!
14. Pray at every opportunity.

How to Engage in Purposeful Habits

Dr. Trahern (Tron)

> "Regardless of WHAT we do in our lives, our WHY—our driving purpose, cause or belief—never changes."
>
> —Simon Sinek

Engaging in purposeful habits begins with our why. Why do we do what we do? Or why do we not do what we need to do? As we set our sails for a life of meaning and purpose, let's first decide where we are going. For some, they are aiming for better relationships. For others, it's financial security or peace of mind and contentment. Whatever goal we decide on, we should reflect on why it is important to us. When we decide what we want to do and be in our life, we must develop an action plan to attain our goals.

I truly believe we were born for a purpose. In the Bible, Jeremiah 29:11 sheds light on our purpose: "For I know the thoughts that I think toward you, saith the Lord, thoughts of peace, and not of evil, to give you an expected end."

This is great news! God has plans for our lives. Although there is a divine plan for our lives, we should pursue habits that align us with God's purpose and plans for our lives.

What are some habits you can cultivate that will inspire you to act?

Here are three action steps to begin your quest to engage in inspiring habits. Firstly, we must slow down and become still. Recently, I visited Fort Lauderdale beach for a time of reflection and relaxation. As I looked at the blue ocean and felt the wind blowing, I sensed a calmness. This inner peace happened because of stilling myself before creation. While there are many mindful practices, I believe those that cause us to reflect on nature and creation ignite inner peace and tranquility.

Secondly, we should still the mind. At times, the mind can race like vehicles on a highway. But stillness of mind can help us slow down and cultivate creative thinking. We must develop habits that inspire us to search out God's plan for our lives.

Thirdly, we should develop a habit of daily gratitude for the blessings given to us. I recommend using a daily journal.

How to Develop Beneficial Habits

Pastor James

Beneficial habits that help to improve our lives and the lives of others. They are the kind of positive habits that we should continue to practice. The key foundational habit that we need to build upon is our relationship with God. Reach out to God in prayer and thoughtful contemplation. Ask God in prayer for knowledge of His will and way for our lives. Next, work on developing a beneficial habit-breaking relationship with oneself.

Start by vowing to respect and honor yourself now. Be open and honest about deficient habits that you need to unpack. What are some known habits that can keep individuals from moving forward in their lives? Here are some examples. Make time for yourself.

Formulate a plan of action for the development of positive relational habits. Then make your personal well-care a priority. Good habits practice leads to positive outcomes. Positive training helps to build a more compelling life. So, we should seek out strategies and techniques for replacing bad habits. Target the bad habit that you want to change. Take small steps and aim at one goal at a time.

1. Make it a morning habit of expressing heartfelt gratitude.
2. Start your day with the focus of the Creator.
3. Start an exercise and relaxation plan and work it.

4. Guard your thought life. Consistently cast away the negative.
5. Practice living in the moment.

Write down an action plan for change. Review your habit change program daily. Do your own self-progress report? When an individual takes part committedly in a growth and change plan, the payoff can be very rewarding.

Positive habits can bring joy and inspiration to daily living through the development and cultivation of enriching habits. Striving for the formation of spiritual habits results in the best meaning and purpose to life. Practice the desired behavior repeatedly. Behavior development and discipline go together.

How to Develop Beneficial Habits

Dr. Trahern (Tron)

> Habit is the intersection of knowledge (what to do), skill (how to do), and desire (want to do).
>
> —Stephen R. Covey

Have you ever desired to do a task but did not act? It can be very challenging to get unstuck from habits that are not serving our purpose.

What are beneficial habits? Beneficial habits are key building blocks that help us establish a solid foundation for success in life. For instance, if a person wants to excel academically, it is vital to develop a foundation of good study habits.

Good habits must be developed early in life. Habits such as discipline, hard work, commitment, and determination are beneficial in working towards objectives. What are some key factors that drive beneficial habits? There are five key areas I believe are necessary for the formation of beneficial habits. These five areas are like pieces of a pie. One must be engaged mentally, emotionally, spiritually, physically, and socially.

The key to developing beneficial habits is to have a strong desire to achieve your goals. When we have strong desires, even if we encounter challenges, we can keep going. Perhaps you would like to lose weight? This begins with a desire to become healthy and well. Once the goal is established, one must get busy working towards it. Perhaps a walk around the block or being more active is a great action step. Maybe changing one's eating habits. To achieve any worthwhile goal, one must be disciplined, committed, work hard, focus, and never give up. Beneficial habits are a choice that one must engage in daily. Start as early as possible to develop good habits. Because the habits that we develop early in life will benefit us in the long run.

Negative Habits in the Family

Pastor James

According to the Mayo Clinic, early childhood experiences may result in misunderstanding, mental health issues, alcohol abuse, drug addiction, and other dysfunctional family issues. This leads to problems in family relationships. So, what is a pathway to resolve such toxic habits?

First, start with communication. Begin to talk to each other. Speak about how important it is to work on breaking generational curses. Breaking generational negative habits of the past serves to create a better future. One generation can aid the next in the removal of past immoral vices.

What are some further issues that cause conflicts among family members? One, ineffective communication can lead to family strife. When family interchange of conversation between people are misunderstood, this can often lead to anger between them. Two, calm down. Perhaps the family can take a break to calm down. Once they are calm, I recommend taking a calm walk to discuss their differences.

Negative Habits in the Family

Dr. Trahern (Tron)

A family that engages in negative habits is one that is lacking in essential areas of development. This includes unmet physical needs, emotional needs, spiritual needs, and social needs.

There are long-term consequences to negative family habits. It affects overall health and well-being. Engaging in negative family habits is like playing a game of tug-of-war. There's constant tension, power struggles, and competition.

Once these habits become ingrained, it takes insight to overcome these negative patterns. Earlier, we discussed Tiffany and Felicity. Due to family conflict, Felicity and Tiffany engaged in unhealthy communication patterns. How could two sisters reared in the same home reach a point of severe conflict? I believe ineffective parenting led to the breakdown in the family structure. When parents have different points of view, it spills over into the parent-child relationship.

How do we break negative family habits?

- Firstly, find a certified counselor trained in family dynamics.
- Secondly, identify a family goal. The goal is a blueprint for overcoming negative patterns.
- Thirdly, practice forgiveness. Learning to forgive can repair damaged relationships.
- Lastly, fairness should be practiced in all interactions among family members.

How to Develop Good Health Habits

Pastor James

Good health and wellness habits mean exercising, eating nutritional foods, and paying attention to mental and spiritual health. When we practice good health habits, we increase our chances of living a longer, healthier life.

The foundation of good health habits begins with eating a nutritional diet, getting plenty of rest, engaging in physical activity, having regular doctor checkups, and engaging in positive spiritual practices. The practice of developing excellent health habits starts with a good health practice plan.

Firstly, do an assessment of negative lifestyle patterns. Create a good health program. Find out what would be an effective and safe exercise regimen just for you. Make it personal. Begin the journey of developing good health habits. Start laying the foundation of consuming nutritional foods. When it comes to establishing better health and habits, begin your day by eating oatmeal.

Secondly, you may want to include organic pancakes, egg whites, and one link of turkey sausage. Drink plenty of water. Keep a display of fruits on your table for a healthy snack. Also, make good food choices for lunch, which include chicken, turkey, beans, nuts, seeds, fruits, and bananas. The abovementioned food items have been proven to add value to wellness.

How to Develop Good Health Habits

Dr. Trahern (Tron)

"Quality is not an act; it is a habit."

— Aristotle

Habits are easy to form but hard to break. Over 2,000 years ago, Aristotle understood that we are the sum of the habits that we develop. We are reaping the fruit of the habits that we have sown. If we want an apple tree, we should plant apple seeds.

Likewise, in our lives, if we want better health, better finances, better relationships, better jobs, better academics, and overall better lives, we must plant the right seeds to produce the harvest that we long for. The moment we decide that we want to be better, we will do better. What are we waiting for?

Many are waiting for the sun to shine. For instance, many are waiting for the right mate. Instead of waiting and looking out the window, begin to work on yourself and take action steps; get out of your comfort zone. To develop good habits, we must break bad habits. The way to break bad habits is to start doing the things that you desire today. If you want to have overall health and wellness, get rid of all your snacks and begin to purchase healthy foods. If you want better relationships, start developing a positive, welcoming attitude. Don't always look on the dark side. Look on the bright side and see the best in others. Here are ten action steps to help you.

1. Start now. Don't wait.
2. Go against resistance and fight the feeling.

Developing Habits that Serve You

3. Wake up every day with an optimistic attitude. Say, "This is the day the Lord has made and I will rejoice and be glad in it."
4. Don't associate with people who reinforce negative habits.
5. Take out the trash of negative thoughts and replace those thoughts with positive thoughts.
6. See yourself being who you've always wanted to be.
7. Be determined. Even if you face obstacles, keep going.
8. Work hard, never give up, and reach for the stars.
9. Affirm that it's not too late to reach your goal and purpose in life.
10. Eradicate fear; believe it is possible.

The Benefits of Exercise

Pastor James

Exercise offers many benefits. Regular exercise improves the cardiovascular system. It reduces stress. Physical activity strengthens muscles and bones. According to the Mayo Clinic, physical exercise benefits: 1. Exercise helps to control weight. 2. Helps to boost energy. 3. Reduces joint inflammation. 4. Lowers blood pressure. 5. Helps you to feel better overall. 6. Helps connect with family and friends.

The goal is to launch a lifelong wellness attitude. Start with a new way of eating.

Firstly, take all unhealthy food out of your cabinet. Secondly, research selections of the healthiest foods.

The Benefits of Exercise

Dr. Trahern (Tron)

According to the Center for Disease Control (CDC), engaging in regular physical activity is one of the most important things you can do for your health. Moreover, they suggested that being physically active can improve your brain health, help manage weight, reduce the risk of disease, strengthen bones and muscles, and improve your ability to do everyday activities.

I feel better today than I did when I was 290 lbs. Even though the weight was necessary for my chosen profession as a professional athlete, today, my health and wellness are better. Many times, people sacrifice their health and wellness for temporary pleasures. Some would argue burgers, French fries, and milkshakes taste good, but they're not going to give the fuel needed for optimal health and wellness. So, what are we waiting for to engage in action steps to help us become physically fit?

Too many generations are suffering needlessly because their parents did not teach them healthy habits. Did you know that a few lifestyle changes in our physical activity can make all the difference? It is not hard to resist delicious pastries. Many times, we eat things and later regret it.

So here are some action steps to help you become more physically well.

Firstly, go to the doctor regularly to get an examination. I was talking to a man who told me he was physically fit externally, but internally, he was suffering. It is important to get blood work and frequent checkups.

Secondly, find out your body mass index. When you lose excessive weight, you're going to feel better. Not only will you have a health boost, but it will also boost your self-esteem. This step is not easy because there are many factors that may contribute to one's weight gain. See your doctor for directions on the best plan that works for you.

Thirdly, develop action plans that work for you. Your action plan can include a walk, a stationary bike ride, an elliptical, weightlifting, strength and conditioning training, resistance training, aerobics, whatever it is we need to start small and develop a plan that's right for you based on your doctor's recommendations.

Effective Spiritual Habits: Spiritual Habits that Enrich Your Life

Pastor James

What are spiritual habits? Spiritual habits are spiritual disciplines that serve to promote mental and physical health. Spiritual activities produce a spiritual experience that helps us to grow and learn how to be a better person. Spiritual exercises also help us to develop more faith in God. Spiritual inner strength is a deep and, importantly, unstoppable belief in yourself. It is more than resilience and the ability to recover. What is the best way to go about developing spiritual strength? From a Christian perspective, strict study of the Bible will produce spiritual strength. Spiritual strength provides the spiritual energy for reaching your objectives.

The habit of planning and setting goals is the best way to develop spiritual habits. Developing spiritual habits can feed our souls and help us grow spiritually. So, what are spiritual habits? Spiritual habits are disciplines that help us to live right. Let us consider some top spiritual habits that can empower us.

1. Live in the moment.
2. Contemplate the existence of God in nature.
3. Appreciate the value of wholeness.
4. Seek the company of friends.
5. Cultivate the virtue of humility.
6. Practice being time sensitive.
7. Be generous in your giving.
8. Help the less fortunate.

9. Read the Bible.
10. Meditate regularly.
11. Pray often.

Effective Spiritual Habits: Spiritual Habits that Enrich Your Life

Dr. Trahern (Tron)

> The degree of our spiritual strength will be in direct proportion to the time we spend in God's Word.
>
> — Elizabeth George

Spiritual strength helps us to endure or bear the load of life. Anyone can say they have spiritual strength when there are no challenges, but when we meet unexpected difficulties, how do we navigate? The most challenging moment of my life was the death of my dear mother. I had to grapple with the reality that her presence was no longer with me. What challenges have you faced? I have learned no one is exempt from the hard knocks of life. Everyone's circumstances and challenges differ, but the commonality is we all will face challenges in life. One's ability to bear the load is my definition of spiritual strength. To effectively bear the load of life, one must spend time with the ultimate load-bearer. The psalmist provided insight into spiritual strength when he said the Lord is the strength of my life. Let us do some self-examination to assess spiritual lives. Do we spend time with our Creator? I have two children now, ages eleven and thirteen, and I enjoy time spent with them. As a father, I understand the importance of having their undivided attention. No electronics, no other distractors, just time with father and sons. Likewise, do you have uninterrupted time with God? Here are some suggestions to strengthen your spiritual life.

1. Give God the best part of your day. When you wake up, spend time meditating.
2. Always have an attitude of gratitude; give thanks for the simple things of life.
3. Spend time in nature to develop an appreciation for things not made with man's hands.
4. Learn to be still; don't be anxious or in a hurry.
5. Encourage others. Because you never know another person's plight.

Chapter 7

Finding a Pathway to Spiritual Enrichment

How to Discover the Spiritually Enlightened Path?

Pastor James

WHAT IS THE PATHWAY TO SPIRITUAL ENRICHMENT?

The path to spiritual enrichment consists of focusing on values, morality, righteousness, faith, virtue, and love, among other enduring principles. Spiritual development begins with an open mind. The individual must decide he or she wants to change. Then, talk to someone who has the kind of spiritual qualities that you want to emulate.

Acknowledge that you are not only a human being, but you are also a spiritual being. It is good to admit that you need a strength stronger than yourself. We need divine power. Do a spiritual inventory to determine your weak traits. Seek out and set up spiritual counseling of interventions for dealing with weak character traits in your personality. Join a competent Christian spiritual group to help with a spiritual enrichment plan. Read popular books and authors on spiritual growth.

Reach out to your Higher Power for assistance and motivation on your journey toward a richer spiritual life. The next thing on our agenda is to work up a spiritual plan for your personal enrichment progress.

Tips for spiritual growth.
1. Start every day by making your request known to God.
2. Express fervent gratitude to the Creator, God.
3. Pray for strength to be intentional. Reach to God in intense prayers daily.
4. Pray for the quality of patience in all you do.
5. Practice being humble and caring in all your daily encounters.
6. Exercise in a daily plan of devotion and meditations. Be consistent in all your spiritual practices.
7. Read the scriptures and other good religious writings.
8. Learn to calm down your mind.
9. See the reality of God in nature.
10. Make smiling a fixed habit.

Practice and learn how to face your adversities, difficulties, and hardships as a pathway toward victory. Learn forgiveness. Try to make past wrongs right. Practice giving your time, talents, and resources to the less fortunate.

What is Spiritual Enrichment?

Dr. Trahern (Tron)

Spiritual enrichment is a person's ability to examine one's life to find out one's purpose for living in the world. In Maslow's highest level of need, he suggested that self-actualization is one's realization of their potential self-fulfillment while seeking personal growth and peak experiences.

In 2003, I stood on Soldier Field in the Windy City of Chicago as a professional football player. It was a rewarding feeling. I had achieved my dream of becoming one of the 26,000 players who have ever played in the National Football League. Although this feeling was exhilarating, I would argue it was not the highest level of self-actualization. I believe self-actualization happened when the door to my dream was closed. When the coach called me in the office and said, "We have to let you go." That was my moment of self-actualization because I had to rebuild my life from the remnants of a broken dream.

Coach's words hit like a whirlwind. Even though I was saddened, within seconds of him releasing me from my job, he said that I would be okay. To me, being okay meant being equipped to handle the loss of a dream and rebuild again. I believe self-actualization helps individuals meet life challenges head-on. Take a moment to reflect on the times in your life when you experienced hardships, but you were able to navigate the challenge. Perhaps you experienced a divorce or a serious illness. Maybe you lost a loved one or a job. Perhaps you're dealing with the challenge of raising a child. Challenges are an inescapable part of life. However, with the right spiritual resources, a positive mindset, and a positive outlook on life, you can overcome.

To illustrate, let's consider a person who is taking a long journey. In order to navigate the journey, the person needs the proper equipment. This journey will include unexpectedness, surprises, and hardships. But because the journeyman is equipped, they can weather the storms of life. Take a moment and reflect on your journey pouch. Do you have the necessary tools to face the twists and turns and storms of life? Let's consider some tools for enriching the path of life.

How to Stay on the Spiritual Path

Pastor James

One must make a committed and dedicated decision to grow and learn. Embark upon the foundation of a new, enriched way of thinking and being. One must become willing to do whatever it takes to grow spiritually. So, what is the pathway of living the spirit of an abundant life of enrichment?

A spiritual enriched path is a positive path of spiritual wholeness and wellness. It is a lifestyle connected to our essential well-being. It is guided by Divine Providence. This is a blueprint undergirded by the guidance of the Holy Scriptures. Therefore, a person must learn to tap into fully embracing the source of faith, commitment, and dedication.

The first step is to open the mind to the possibility of navigating life on a higher plane. This process starts with surrendering your will to God or your Higher Power.

Realize that supreme guidance is needed by everyone. In fact, we are all needy creatures. We are unable to make this life journey alone. The question is, how can we plant our feet upon the spiritual enriched path and stay on it? Set your goal. Do what it takes to reach your purpose. Learn about different forms of spiritual disciplines that can empower you on your pathway of personal growth.

Through outreach programs, you can connect with other encouragers. Decide what religious values and principles support your morals. Get started.

1. Ask for steadfast faith and grace in continuing the unwavering faith journey toward spiritual enrichment.
2. Do an inward nourishing through prayer and meditation as often as possible.
3. Begin a careful study plan of the Bible, religious books, and other spiritual research. For example, the Bible says to study to show yourself approved unto God.
4. Start a time of study each day to get to know God better.
5. Join a faith-based community fellowship.
6. Assemble with your fellowship according to scheduled times.
7. Do your part in supporting and promoting the spiritual principles of the fellowship.
8. Cultivate a desire for growth.
9. Work hard to stay true to the principle of your religious course of action. Make it a practice.
10. Cultivate an attitude of spiritual sensitivity.
11. Make it a practice of living a life of service to others.
12. Develop a life of service through divine love.

How to Stay on the Spiritual Path

Dr. Trahern (Tron)

Life is full of uncertainties and challenges, twists, and turns. With all the challenges that we have to face, how can we stay on the spiritual path? This requires discipline, commitment, effort, faith, and determination.

Growing up in the inner city of Fort Lauderdale, I was always intrigued by those who were able to resist drugs, temptation, alcohol, and distractions to achieve a worthy goal. It always saddened me to see athletes who made it out of the inner city, but bad choices and paths led them down the wrong road. I believe spiritual enrichment helps a person navigate the pitfalls of life because their focus on their goal brings purpose and meaning to their lives.

When we are enthusiastic, having God within the winds and pressures of life does not deter us from our dreams. Many begin the race of life, but due to distractions, they fall out of the race. So, when one decides to pursue a goal of being a good parent, a good student, a good employee, a good player, or whatever the predetermined goal, there must be focus in order to reach the goal.

Here are some suggestions to help an individual stay on the right spiritual path.

1. Set a goal to grow spiritually.
2. Identify potential distractions that can hinder spiritual growth. When one decides to plant a garden, the soil is cultivated, and anything that can hinder growth is removed. Likewise, when we want to grow spiritually, we must identify potential people, places, or things that can block spiritual growth.
3. Associate with the right people. Negative people can hinder spiritual progress; therefore, we need to choose our associates wisely.
4. Remain focused. To grow, we must have laser focus and not allow external or internal distractions to impede our progress.
5. Keep a positive attitude. Maintaining a positive attitude can be compared to fuel in our tank. When we have proper fuel, we can go the distance. Therefore, every day, we need solid practices to help us to have a positive mental attitude.
6. Turn setbacks into opportunities. We cannot afford to let the setbacks of life hinder us from spiritual growth. When I lost my dream job, I had to rebuild with remnants of what was left. When we set out for a goal, there are going to be obstacles and challenges, but we have to continue to drive and move forward towards our dreams and goals.

What Is Spiritual Enrichment?

Pastor James

Spiritual enrichment is the supernatural endowment of gifts from on high. It gives us the power to do good on Earth. It is the process of continued spiritual growth.

Enrichment, with power from on high, can carry light to a world blighted by discord. Spiritual formation is a human need; it is fundamental to well-being. It is said that spirituality is the bedrock for sustaining stewardship, compassion, care, and concern for humanity. We need it. So, what are the fruits of spiritual enhancement?

Firstly, the mind becomes fortified with the spirit of love. When the mind is enhanced with love, the mind moves towards a lifestyle of hope and peace. The peace and hope God bestows upon the believer is lasting. In John 14:27, it says, "Peace I leave with you, my peace I give unto you: not as the world giveth, give I unto you. Let not your heart be troubled, neither let it be afraid."

Secondly, spiritual development is the greatest wealth that a person can pursue. Spiritual growth provides us with the quality of life we long for. This is the power that relieves the persistence of anxiety, fear, worry, discouragements, and other emotional maladies. On the pathway of life, our soul often craves calmness in the face of life's challenges. Spirituality fosters a greater sense of well-being. Spiritual enrichment aids one in living a more positive and meaningful life. Practicing spiritual empowerment principles energizes one's drive and pursuit of goals. In Jeremiah 29:11, it says, "For I know the thoughts that I think toward you, saith the Lord, thoughts of peace, and not of evil, to give you an expected end." God knows the purpose and plan He has for you. Fortitude is another great value that comes with spiritual growth. Fortitude is the ability to commit to God despite temptations that may confront us. The scripture put it this way: if you be led by the Spirit, you will not give into the ploy of the flesh.

Divine power is an enabling force. In Acts 1:8, it says, "But ye shall receive power, after that the Holy Ghost is come upon you." God promises us the empowerment of the Spirit to spread hope to others. This power is available to all people if you can discover it, but you must seek it. It pays to pursue it at great cost.

The payoff of spiritual improvement deals with knowledge and awareness about the various roles we must play in life. Enrichment provides practical insights on how to navigate life in the productive course of living.

Spiritual enrichment is movement toward a closer connection with God. It is about developing deeper meaning and understanding about how to get along in life.

Divine strength exceeds human strength. This is the kind of power that enables one to keep moving forward in a principled manner. It is a practice that offers ongoing, continuous treatment for help and comfort. The spiritual development plan stimulates the practice of activities such as prayer, meditation, and yoga. Exercise of these actions promotes our total well-being. You must acquire it. So, receive and own it. The gospel gives us strength. How does spiritual enrichment help us? Spiritual fortification helps us to live disciplined lives.

Spiritual strength in Psalm 28:7: The Lord is my strength and my shield; my heart trusted in him, and I am helped: therefore, my heart greatly rejoiceth; and with my song will I praise him.

My heart leaps for joy, and with my song I praise him. Guess what, God gives divine power to all believers.

In Ephesians 3:4-19, it says:

4 Whereby, when ye read, ye may understand my knowledge in the mystery of Christ.

5 Which in other ages was not made known unto the sons of men, as it is now revealed unto his holy apostles and prophets by the Spirit;

6 That the Gentiles should be heirs, and of the same body, and partakers of his promise in Christ by the gospel:

7 Whereof I was made a minister, according to the gift of the grace of God given unto me by the effectual working of his power.

8 Unto me, who am less than the least of all saints, is this grace given, that I should preach among the Gentiles the unsearchable riches of Christ;

⁹ And to make all men see what is the fellowship of the mystery, which from the beginning of the world hath been hid in God, who created all things by Jesus Christ:

¹⁰ To the intent that now unto the principalities and powers in heavenly places might be known by the church the manifold wisdom of God,

¹¹ According to the eternal purpose which he purposed in Christ Jesus our Lord:

¹² In whom we have boldness and access with confidence by the faith of him.

¹³ Wherefore I desire that ye faint not at my tribulations for you, which is your glory.

¹⁴ For this cause, I bow my knees unto the Father of our Lord Jesus Christ,

¹⁵ Of whom the whole family in heaven and Earth is named,

¹⁶ That he would grant you, according to the riches of his glory, to be strengthened with might by his Spirit in the inner man;

¹⁷ That Christ may dwell in your hearts by faith; that ye, being rooted and grounded in love,

¹⁸ May be able to comprehend with all saints what is the breadth, and length, and depth, and height;

¹⁹ And to know the love of Christ, which passeth knowledge, that ye might be filled with all the fulness of God.

In Isaiah 12:2, it says, *"Behold, God is my salvation; I will trust, and not be afraid: for the Lord Jehovah is my strength and my song; he also is become my salvation."*

Power for conviction, courage, and comfort to remove what we cannot remove in our own power.

Mark 11:22 *And Jesus answering saith unto them, Have faith in God.*

Why is spirituality important? Spirituality is important because it touches all areas of life that affect wellness. It impacts happiness and comfort, hope, love, and all phases of the human experience.

How does the acquisition of spiritual power begin?

Spiritual strength starts with communing with God. Through prayer and meditation from within. These exercises help us to connect with the God of the universe.

Here are your wisdom verses:

Psalm 23

[1] The Lord is my shepherd; I shall not want

[2] He maketh me to lie down in green pastures: he leadeth me beside the still waters.

[3] He restoreth my soul: he leadeth me in the paths of righteousness for his name's sake.

[4] Yea, though I walk through the valley of the shadow of death, I will fear no evil: for thou

> *art with me; thy rod and thy staff they comfort me.*
>
> *⁵ Thou preparest a table before me in the presence of mine enemies: thou anointest my head with oil; my cup runneth over.*
>
> *⁶ Surely goodness and mercy shall follow me all the days of my life: and I will dwell in the house of the Lord forever.*

> Colossians 2:19 *And not holding the Head, from which all the body by joints and bands having nourishment ministered, and knit together, increaseth with the increase of God.*

> John 17:3 *And this is life eternal, that they might know thee the only true God, and Jesus Christ, whom thou hast sent.*

Spiritual strength does not come easy. In life, we need physical, emotional, mental, and spiritual strength, but spiritual strength is far more important. Why is this true?

Spiritual Strength — What is it? It is your greatest power.

> Eph 3:20 *Now unto him that is able to do exceeding abundantly above all that we ask or think, according to the power that worketh in us*

Holy Ghost power helps us meet the challenges of life. You must remember that life is filled with challenges. Life is also designed with challenges to test a person's faith and resilience and shapes them into the best person that they can be.

> James 1:1-5
>
> *"¹ James, a servant of God and of the Lord Jesus Christ, to the twelve tribes which are scattered abroad, greetings.*
>
> *² My brethren, count it all joy when ye fall into diverse temptations.*
>
> *³ Knowing this, that the trying of your faith worketh patience.*
>
> *⁴ But let patience have her perfect work, that ye may be perfect and entire, wanting nothing.*
>
> *⁵ If any of you lack wisdom, let him ask of God, that giveth to all men liberally, and upbraideth not; and it shall be given him."*

What is spiritual strength? For the joy of the Lord is your strength.

> Nehemiah 8:10 *We need it. It is unshakable power for now and the future.*
>
> Acts 1:8 *But ye shall receive power, after that the Holy Ghost is come upon you:*

Where does spiritual strength come from?

Glory to God in the church! Glory to God in the Messiah, in Jesus! Glory down all the generations! Glory through all millennia! Oh, yes!

What is the importance of spiritual strength? It gives the believer peace.

The gospel satisfies our greatest longing.

> Romans 8:15-16 *For ye have not received the spirit of bondage again to fear; but ye have received the Spirit of adoption, whereby we cry, Abba, Father.*
>
> *^{16} The Spirit itself beareth witness with our spirit, that we are the children of God:*

The power of God to save.

Romans 1:16-17

^{16} For I am not ashamed of the gospel of Christ: for it is the power of God unto salvation to every one that believeth; to the Jew first, and also to the Greek.

^{17} For therein is the righteousness of God revealed from faith to faith: as it is written, The just shall live by faith.

1 John 2:1

"My little children, these things write I unto you, that ye sin not. And if any man sin, we have an advocate with the Father, Jesus Christ the righteous."

Consider some ways our faith helps others.

- ☞ Helps burdens.
- ☞ Helps with opposition.
- ☞ Helps us to help others.
- ☞ Enables us to persevere.
- ☞ Helps to resist temptation.

What are some spiritual strengths?
1. We chase after the word of God. 1 Peter 2:3 Now that you have tasted that the Lord is good."
2. Positively grounded
3. Action-oriented power
4. High motivation
5. Courage under pressure
6. Unwavering, bold, and dynamic

A strong, vigorous determination that is confident and well-established. Spiritual power renders the faithful steadfast and ready for anything. Philippians 4:13 says, "I can do all things through Christ which strengthen me." Spiritual strength is a character strength that works from the inside out.

So, how do we build spiritual strength? Psalm 138: Seek the Lord by prayer so that you won't fall into temptation. Spiritual strength provides power.

Benefits of spiritual strength: equips and empowers and makes the believer more serviceable in the world. Acts 1:8 *"But ye shall receive power, after that the Holy Ghost is come upon you: and ye shall be witnesses unto me both in Jerusalem, and in all Judaea, and in Samaria, and unto the uttermost part of the earth."* It also fills the believer, more importantly, with a wealth of spiritual fruit. Isaiah 12:2 "Behold, God is my salvation; I will trust, and not be afraid: for the LORD JEHOVAH is my strength and my song; he also is become my salvation."

What Is Spiritual Enrichment?

Dr. Trahern (Tron)

> "When one door of happiness closes, another opens; but often we look so long at the closed door that we do not see the one which has been opened for us."
>
> — HELEN KELLER

Spiritual enrichment is the inner strength, courage, faith, and belief to carry on when the doors of our dreams are shut. When the door shut on my NFL dream, I quickly searched for the doors of possibility. Dr. Schuller encouraged us to have the possibility of thinking to continue to move forward in the face of challenges. Have you stared at the door of discouragement too long? Do you know that God has a purpose and plan for your life? Life is full of possibilities, but we must discover the path to spiritual enrichment.

How do we discover the path to reaching our God-given potential? This is not easy. It can be fearful. It can be stressful and anxiety-provoking to discover the right path. So, what do we do when we face the crossroads of life? How do we get on the path of spiritual enrichment that leads to our possibilities? First, we must believe in God and believe in ourselves. This belief is necessary to increase our self-esteem and self-worth. When we feel good about ourselves, it gives us enthusiasm for living our best life. According to *Enjoying the Journey*, the word "enthusiasm" comes from two Greek words: en and theos, or God within. When we know that God is within us, it helps us deal with the difficulties of life.

When God is within us, empowering us, it doesn't exempt us from the blows and the hardships of life. But He becomes a compass or GPS to help us reach our destination. Perhaps you are off course today because you're not guided by your internal GPS or compass. It's not too late to discover the right path. It's within your reach. We mustn't let the blows of life crush our spirits. We must keep the burning fire within. You must let your passion drive your success. When we are passionate about our dreams or goals, it will drive us to be successful.

Chapter 8

Closeness

Pastor James

How do we create closeness in relationships? We can start by fostering trust, acceptance, and honesty and setting aside time to talk openly. Additionally, we should make all our conversations encouraging and positive. Look for the good in and highlight the humanity in everyone. The Bible puts it this way: be kind, for everyone you meet is fighting a hard battle. We can contribute closeness to our families by being kind, respectful, and helpful to everyone. Attractive lips speak kind words.

How to Create Closeness in the Family

Creating closeness in the extended family begins with you. Try to understand the various family functions at different levels. So, learning to accept each member as who they are can be a bridge to closeness.

Love and empathy are the fundamental components for strengthening family bonds. Clearly communicate to the family the love that you have for them. Show empathy by opening up and sharing experiences. Withhold judgments and avoid being critical. Frequently say, "I love you." Don't wait for family to call you. Be willing to be the first to reach out. Write notes or send emails expressing positive feelings. Initiate family get-togethers. Some family members may respond negatively, so don't take it personally. If you are willing to take down, there is a better chance of reaching the desired outcome. Flexibility and compromise can foster closeness.

Learn how to celebrate extended family members. Convey to the family the importance of passing down good family traditions.

1. Focus on intimacy. Be emotionally intelligent. Seek to be caring and considerate about each other's feelings. Accept the broad range of differences within the family system. Create opportunities for growth.
2. Do fun things together like family cookouts.
3. Create chat lines.
4. Try to create a culture of love, respect, and honesty, and make attempts to show that you care by actions. Actions speak louder than words.
5. Share material things.
6. Work at developing a deeper appreciation for each other.
7. Open channels of communication that can help settle contentions differences.
8. Attack the problem, not the person.
9. Be aware of your emotions.

In summary, the goal is to minimize or reduce the amount of contention in the family system. Progress toward conflict resolution can be accomplished through empathy, love, understanding, humility, and insight. The scriptures contain timeless principles for reaching such goals. For instance, Romans 12:9 says, "Let love be without dissimulation. Abhor that which is evil; cleave to that which is good. 10 Be kindly affectioned one to another with brotherly love; in honor preferring one another."

Love is important in our lives because it promotes closeness in our relationships. Loving one another should be our chief aim in life. We are on this planet to spread the idea of love and the beauty of closeness.

Dr. Trahern (Tron)

How to Create Closeness in Relationships?

"We can improve our relationships with others by leaps and bounds if we become encouragers instead of critics."

— Joyce Meyer

Relationships are a priceless commodity. Sure, yeah, but many times, people undervalue human relationships and place more value on things that lack eternal value. As Maya Angelou said, people will forget what you did, but people will never forget how you made them feel.

Let us begin this chapter by doing some self-reflection. When people meet you and leave your presence, what would you want them to say about you? Will they say you were warm and caring? Perhaps they will say you are enthusiastic and full of joy, or they may say you are loving and inspire them. If we want honey, Dale Carnegie said we can't kick over the beehive. Many of us want sweet relationships, but we're kicking the beehive, and we're getting stung instead of experiencing the sweetness of the honeycomb.

After working with married couples and families for over a decade, I've learned that words are powerful. The things we say can uplift others or leave a sour taste in their mouth.

Let's reflect on our vignette on the life of Tony. Tony was seventeen years old when his friends introduced him to marijuana. His friends offered marijuana as a solution to the problems of life. What if Tony was equipped with the life skills to resist peer pressure? If the bond between his family and future goals had been stronger, marijuana would have been crowded out. I believe many relationships suffer because individuals treat each other poorly. In my counseling experience, often those who are hurting respond to life based on the feelings they are dealing with. For instance, Tony, because of the feelings and emotions of sadness and loss of purpose, turned to peers for acceptance and drugs as a temporary fix to help him with the challenges of life.

But if he had close, intimate connections, life would be different. Would you like for things to be different in your relationships? Would you like to enjoy more closeness and intimacy? Would you like to experience more satisfaction?

It's possible, but we must make the right investments in our relationship. People invest in 401Ks, 403 (b's), but often, we don't make the proper investments in our relationships. Perhaps a father needs to spend less time at the office and more time investing in his children. Maybe the mother who only sees what the child is not doing should focus on what the child is doing. The couple that has been together for years, whose relationship is drifting apart, needs to find what brought them together in the first place.

Life is not about what we see; it is about how we see. We often are looking out of the wrong lenses. We can always exchange our out-of-focus lens for one that's clearer. My job as a counselor is to give people a new set of ocular relational lenses to help them see people from a different perspective. We see as we are; therefore, when we change ourselves, we can see others from a different perspective.

So, how does relational closeness happen? It happens when we become intentional about our relationships.

Here are some action steps to help you create more intimacy in your relationship.

1. Instead of criticizing, be an encourager. Learn to identify what is working and not what isn't working.
2. Make amends with past hurts and failures. Many times, the roadblocks of past ails block relational progress.
3. Communicate effectively. Often, it's important for us to over-communicate rather than under-communicate.
4. Don't assume. Building relationships on assumptions is like building a house on sand. It won't stand.
5. Offer gifts. Gifts can be given small and great. A kind gesture in a relationship goes a long way. Find out what's important to another person and be intentional about offering that gift. It doesn't always have to be monetary; it's the thought that counts.
6. Love is not a feeling; it is an act. Love is action. It's not based on feeling. We don't love because we feel like it. We love unconditionally because it's the right thing to do. John 3:15 talks about God's love for mankind. As we let His love spill over into our lives, we have love that will spill over into the lives of others.

How to Create Closeness in the Family

Pastor James

We can start by doing some research on our family identity. As we research and explore family traditions and values, this discovery can lead to the enrichment of the family unit.

Merging closeness in the family requires effort and commitment. One must reconcile that closeness in family relationships is a human need. It is not something that just happens. It is something that must be cultivated.

Creating closeness in the extended family begins with you. Try to understand that various family members function at different levels. So, when we learn to become accepting of each member as who they are, we can show empathy by offering help in a time of need. Just by being there for a family is a strong sign of compassion. Sharing good thoughts and positive affirmations can be a bridge to closeness.

Love and empathy are the fundamental components for strengthening family bonds. So clearly communicate to the family the love that you have for them. Show appreciation by opening up and sharing experiences. Withhold judgments and avoid being critical. Frequently say, "I love you." Don't wait for family to call you. Be willing to be the first to reach. Write notes or send emails expressing positive feelings. Initiate family get-togethers. Some family members may respond negatively, but don't take it personally. If you are willing to take down , there is a better chance of reaching the desired outcome. Flexibility and compromise can foster closeness from members who may feel a level of disconnection. Another positive consideration for bringing family members closer is by sharing family traditions.

Learn how to celebrate extended family members by gathering them under one roof during holidays. These celebrations are excellent times to reminisce or convey to the family the importance of passing down good family traditions.

Below are listed techniques for creating closeness in the family.

1. Focus on intimacy. Be emotionally intelligent. Seek to be caring and considerate about each other's feelings. Accept the broad range of differences within the family system. Create opportunities for growth.
2. Do fun things together like family cookouts.
3. Create chat lines.
4. Try to create a culture of love, respect, honesty, and make attempts to show that you care by actions. Actions speak louder than words.
5. Share material things.
6. Moral and sentimental ties and nurture.
7. Work at developing a deeper appreciation for each other.
8. Open channels of communication that can help settle contentions differences.
9. Attack the problem, not the person.

10. Be aware of your emotions.

In summary, the goal is to minimize or reduce the amount of contention in the family system. Progress toward conflict resolution can be accomplished through empathy, love, understanding, humility, and insight. The scriptures contain timeless principles for reaching such goals. For instance, Romans 12:9-10.

Love is important in our lives because it promotes closeness in our relationships. Loving one another should be our chief aim in life. We are on this plane to spread the idea of love and the beauty of closeness.

How to Create Closeness in the Family

Dr. Trahern (Tron)

Families come in all shapes and sizes. Families are unique. While families can be a source of strength and stability, they can also be places of conflict and emotional upheaval. Therefore, making a family work harmoniously requires a collective effort.

So, how do we create closeness in family relationships? According to Psychcentral.com, there are four types of closeness in family relationships: physical intimacy, emotional intimacy, intellectual intimacy, and spiritual intimacy. Physical closeness consists of hugs, touches, and physical closeness. Emotional closeness is when individuals share their deepest feelings. Intellectual closeness is when one shares one's deep thoughts and opinions in a mutual way. Spiritual intimacy is where one shares their deepest ideas about life's purpose and meaning as it relates to the divine source.

To apply these concepts, I will revisit the scenario of George. George is seventeen years old, and he lacks closeness with his family of origin. George has made decisions that have violated his parents' trust. As a result, there is tension in the family.

Family conflict and tension can be likened to the raging waters of the sea. The troubled water consists of life challenges, hardships, and difficulties. The question is, how do we navigate life's waters without sinking or drowning in problems?

Consider George. He is stuck in a problem. He wants to make changes, but he doesn't see his possibility. He feels estranged from his family and hopeless. In the past, when he went to therapy, it failed to bridge the gaps of the relationship. He left the sessions feeling more confused because he was blamed for the problem.

Have you ever felt misunderstood in a relationship? Have you ever tried to fix a problem, but it appeared to get worse? Have you ever felt like you were treading the waters of conflict?

Perhaps many youths feel this way; they're living in homes, and they feel misunderstood. How do we reconcile relationship problems? I have worked with countless parents who feel overwhelmed and stressed in their parenting. A parent cannot be effective when they are depleted or burned out. In sports, when a player is tired during a competition, a good coach will call for a timeout to refresh. It's amazing how this happens in sports, but it often doesn't happen in relationships.

George's struggle happened when he was a preteen. But his parents did not seek help until he was out of control. Sadly, his parents ignored all the warning signs. As a caregiver, it is vital to give attention to warning signs and take proper actions to get your teen the help they need.

Bridging the Gaps in Family Relationships

Pastor James

Healing the divide from past generations is a vital consideration. We must get started. Transformation of relationships will require discipline. But it is worth the effort so that all members can be supported. This will require removing the divide that blocks closeness in family relations. Differences among family members over time lead to longstanding gaps in closeness. What are some actions and attitudes that cause divisions in family systems? For example, conduct related to religion, affluence, anger, social status, marriage, toxicity, dislike, and emotional traits of individuals.

What is family disunity? It is a relationship where some members continuously feel attacked, demeaned, misunderstood, and unsupported. When such a pattern of emotional habits is left to foster, they will result in even greater toxic relations. These types of toxic dynamics will require intervention. Behaviors such as arguments, silent treatment, envy, and attempting to win arguments at all costs are also signs of toxicity in family systems. These negative qualities lead to entrenched features in family units that can cause frustration, distress, hurt, and emotional pain. Sometimes even one toxic member can weave lies that can cause toxicity in ten other family members or more. So, what are some useful tips for closing the gaps of disunity in family systems? Some families are organizing counseling group sessions to discuss family differences.

Therefore, it is vital that we become more passionate and hopeful about closing the gap in flawed family relationships. Let us explore some wholesome methods for improving the divide that happens in far too many family systems. I will seek to pull out some proven fundamental principles that have proven to work in the past in creating closer family bonds.

The Book of Proverbs in the Bible points out several verses that emphasize instructions on harmony in the home. When there is beauty in the character, there is harmony in the home. In Psalms 133:1, this scripture verse offers great wisdom about harmony in the family. "How good and pleasant it is when God's people live together in unity" (NIV). What does this mean? We can pray for peace in the family. Family connection is a key part of the wisdom of the scriptures concerning 1 Peter 3:8: Finally, be ye all of one mind, having compassion one of another, love as brethren, be pitiful, be courteous: In 1 Peter 3:8, the verse means to allow true love to govern your life. Love others with the same kind of love you would like bestowed upon you.

How can we begin to bridge the gap in family relationships?

1. Communication is the best way of starting the process of healing the division that often occurs in family systems.
2. Agree to disagree without becoming disagreeable. Pledge to respect each other's feelings and opinions.
3. Open conversation or interactions with honest dialogue.
4. Honor past generational bonds.
5. Think about and talk about bonds in previous generations.
6. Acceptance means living with and valuing differences in other family members.
7. Trips: Family vacations are a good way to strengthen family ties and are often highly beneficial endeavors.
8. Commonality yields positive cohesion.
9. Empathy and emotional ties: empathy is a dynamic force that can be used to bring family members closer.
10. Understanding each other's roles and boundaries can facilitate the mending and repairing of damaged relations. As good family members, let us work together restoring the broken family breech. But let us take heed of how we are building because this time, we want to fortify the gap in the wall.

It Is the Season to Build!

Bridging the Gaps in Family Relationships

Dr. Trahern (Tron)

Building bridges is essential to family relationships. The fact that a bridge needs to be built suggests that there is a relational divide. For instance, when there is a problem in a relationship, it often reveals itself in interactional patterns. People begin to distance themselves from each other, and tensions begin to rise. Therefore, a bridge is necessary to avoid sinking in the troubled waters of the relation.

Perhaps there is a lack of trust in your relationship. A well-constructed bridge can strengthen the relationship between two parties. Why is a relational bridge necessary? Because conflicts exist, and they have a table in life. The relational bridge is a metaphor that helps to strengthen connections and maintain relational bonds. In Tiffany and Felicity's vignette, there is a divide that can only be created by building strong bridges. How do we build these bridges? Strong and lasting bridges are built through trust, intimacy, love, joy, faith and connections.

Here are some action steps you can take to repair your relationship. Essentially you are creating a bridge to strengthen your connection to the person who you are at odds with.

1. Awareness that a change needs to happen. As a counselor, when I observe certain behavioral responses, such as isolation and criticism, that is a symptom of a deeper need. Therefore, my focus is to treat the problem that created the divide.

2. A willingness to let go. It has been said that the windshield is larger than the rearview mirror for a purpose. Many times, we look at what was small and insignificant in the past rather than at the bigger picture of what is ahead of us. To build relational bridges, let's begin to look at the big picture. Let us live with no regrets. This is an active choice to not hold a grudge against someone. Although this is not easy, it's better for your overall health and wellness.
3. Focus on the positive and create through emotional closeness. Develop a fondness or affection. Identify strengths the person possesses as opposed to focusing on their weaknesses.

Finally, follow the golden rule of treating others how you want to be treated. I have observed individuals planting seeds of bitterness, anger, and resentment, hoping to get a harvest of love, enjoyment, and peace. Let us plant the right seeds so we can reap the right harvest.

Chapter 9

Build Relationship Bonds

Pastor James

Quality time, communication, respect, teamwork, and appreciation are the bedrock for bringing family members closer. Closing the gap in the clan can start with one person with a plan.

How do we approach building bonds in family relationships? How do we create connections in the family system? The most important thing about the family unit is closeness. The close bonds in a family system require love, joy, peace, and satisfaction from the group. What are some ways of creating closeness in the tribe?

Here are some effective tips for reconciliation in the divided family structure:

1. Listen to each member of the family attentively, even if they speak negatively.
2. Give a gift to people who may feel that they are being overlooked in the family.
3. Plan a gathering or adventure trip for the entire family. Make everyone feel welcome.

Entertain thoughts from everyone on how to continue bonding with the family. Keep increasing listening skills until everyone can be heard without being contradicted.

The Bible teaches that we need to do whatever we can to strengthen ties in the family. In 1 Timothy 5:8, we are encouraged to care for our families.

"In every conceivable manner, the family is link to our past, bridge to our future."

Alex Haley

Strengthening family bonds means creating a deeper connection between family members and deepening the bonds of love, respect, trust, and understanding. It can involve activities that bring the family together such as shared meals, game nights, or outings.

Fight to bring and hold the family together.

Dr. Trahern (Tron)

> "The happiest moments of my life have been the few which I have passed at home in the bosom of my family."
>
> —Thomas Jefferson

Building strong family connections is essential. When family bonds are strong, each family member feels safe and secure. Developing strong family bonds requires time and effort by all members. When family connections are strong, they guard against unhealthy dynamics.

For instance, earlier we discussed Tiffany and Felicity's relationship. How could two sisters who grew up in the same home with both parents become estranged?

What caused the dark clouds of tension and jealousy to arise? It all started in early childhood. Tiffany perceived that her sister received better treatment than she did. These bottled-up emotions of bitterness begin to fester and spill over into Tiffany's work and personal life. It was like the venom of a poison snake bite that went all through her system. Like the venom that interferes with functioning after the bite happens, Tiffany's bitterness was spreading throughout her system. It was affecting her thinking, emotions, and affection for her family. She was in desperate need of treatment. I have witnessed countless clients carrying burdens from the past. The masses of these burdens fracture the foundation of relationships in marriages and family relationships.

I believe all people long for connection at the deepest level. But Tiffany created a narrative where she did not get what she deserved. It's like a mother giving birth but failing to provide proper nourishment to the child. Instead of wholesome, pure milk, watered-down formula was given.

This was the case with Tiffany. She was nourishing her mind and emotions with unhealthy thinking habits. She was telling herself: I am worthless, a mishap, and I don't have value. Sadly, she hid these feelings from everyone until one day, she exploded at work. Her outburst was likened to a can of soda that had been shaken up and left in the heat of the sun. When her feelings were out in the open, they affected everyone within reach.

Tiffany's narrative could have been altogether different if she had sought help at the first sign of unfairness and jealousy.

What if the parents had given more attention to her nonverbals and emotional withdrawal? Tiffany longed and thirsted for a strong attachment to her mom and dad.

What is a strong, secure attachment?

I believe a strong, secure attachment happens in environments where one feels loved and accepted. Strong family bonds are created through intentional acts of love and kindness.

This is best illustrated in the words of Paul in the scripture. He said, "Love is patient and kind. Love is not jealous or boastful or proud or rude. It does not demand its own way. It is not irritable, and it keeps no record of being wronged. It does not rejoice about injustice but rejoices whenever the truth wins out. Love never gives up, never loses faith, is always hopeful, and endures through every circumstance."

What if all societal families showed the type of love listed above? We would have a better world. We would have fewer Tiffanys in the world. Although she had two parents in the home, they lacked the insight to give all their children what they needed. Every child needs to belong, even if they have interests that are not the parents' preference.

What Is Building Relational Bonds in Family Relationships?

Pastor James

Building relationships bonds is about applying healing balm to your relationships. Encourage all family members to discuss their thoughts and feelings freely. Come up with some traditions that celebrate the strength and support of your family tree. Take into consideration that the moral and ethical values traditionally held and passed on from past generations are valuable.

Loving and caring for all our family will compel us to participate in building bridges for connecting the family. Learn, grow, and be determined to render the best service for closing the gaps in your family relations.

Shared passions, interests and values, unwavering commitment, acts of kindness, positive qualities, and impactful qualities help to the community.

Family bonds are an essential part of closing the gap in family relationships. It is a way of supporting one another and showing approval for each other. It helps to remember both the good times and bad times. Think about where you started and how far you have come in life. Appreciate those family members who offered you encouragement and kindness. Think about the hardships and struggles that you faced and what you learned from them.

It can be rewarding to ask about the path that many of your ancestors traveled, hoping for a better future for their offspring. Such scrutiny can foster strength for bonding family relationships. The Bible says to stand at the crossroads of life, and ask for the old pathway, and when you find it, walk therein Jeremiah 6:16.

What are some other pathways to building bonds in family relationships? A key to building secure bonds in our relationships is to make investing in your relations a priority—six ways to strengthen relationships and build bonds.

1. Sponsor family gatherings and thank everyone for coming together. Express how wonderful it is to have an opportunity to get to know each other better. Encourage each member not to wait for a phone call. Continue to call each other.
2. Try to engage with all people.
3. Smile and give everyone a chance to be heard.
4. Formulate a mission statement.
5. At home, make it a priority to share meals together. Do chores together. Create time for hobbies. Always listen to each other attentively. Make good eye contact. Make this a practice.
6. Recognize that all people are emotional beings. Not everyone functions at the same level. So be caring and empathetic.

What Is Building Relational Bonds in Family Relationships?

Dr. Trahern (Tron)

Many years ago, I traveled to Key West. For the first time, I drove across the seven-mile bridge for a high school football game. It was an amazing experience. The structure was fascinating. The engineers were able to create this massive bridge. This bridge connects the Keys on multiple levels, both high and low. It took ingenuity to create such a massive structure. Sadly, many times, we spend more time on structures than we do on human relationships. What if we took time to build and invest in our relationships? What if parents invested more time in their children? Whether they took time to understand their world or not, it's our life from their child's perspective. What if more children saw life from their parents' perspective? What if siblings worked together effectively? What are the theories of common bonds that caused them to share with each other? Where the husband and wife were aligned with each other's goals, dreams, and aspirations. Where the communication was a two-way role that allowed a give-and-take exchange. If this were the case, families would experience more harmoniousness, and there would be stronger connections. In my experience as a counselor, many issues have happened because of misunderstandings and assumptions. I believe it is vital to look at life from the lens of the other person.

Have you ever got in a verbal disagreement later to discover that you were all wrong? It's like building a house on sand because we have assumed our foundation is faulty. Therefore, for us to have or build strong bonds, we must have understanding, compassion, commitment, love, trust, knowledge, and hope. When we apply these essential qualities to our relationship, strong bridges will be created to help build stronger connections.

Building Marriage Bonds

Pastor James

Marriage bonds must be cultivated. Christianity today is about love and marriage. Strong marriages do not automatically happen. They require commitment and investment. The key to marriage enrichment is doing positive things together. Praying together is a positive game changer that strengthens the marriage connection. It is said the family that prays together remains together. So, it is profitable to consistently pray together for the betterment of the marriage bond.

What does building marriage bonds mean? Marriage bonds are the commitments, pledges, and moral principles that hold marriages together in a reciprocal way. Marriage is a legal and spiritual union between two people. Marriage is about a committed bond based on the principles of giving and receiving. The union is based on mutual respect.

How can lasting bonds be cultivated in marriage? This will require devotion and loyalty. It takes effort to cultivate the process of growth. Each partner must take a creative approach to the enrichment of the marriage. Creating strong, lasting ties depends on a commitment to the loyalty of the value that each person places on the relationship.

For change to evolve, you must determine that it is time for change. Then, make the change happen. You must do the work. Now, set a course of action for the process. Your desire must be fueled by passion. This kind of relationship is motivated by a

Build Relationships Bonds

mutual exchange of support, love, and concern. A mutually complementary relationship must be shared as a connection. The sharing of obligation should be dependent upon the ability and strength of the married couple.

Along with friendship and transparency, other key factors in establishing a strong foundation in marriage are open communication and honesty. Marriage requires a lot of knowledge and understanding. Continue to explore strategies for bolstering your marriage.

What are some tips for creating stronger bonds in your marriage relationship?

1. Start with the determination that you will keep building your marriage relationship on mutual love and respect.
2. Start every day by asking God for divine guidance to honor your relationships.
3. Engage in some kind of daily activity that will help you become a better person.
4. Be willing to compromise. Be willing to take down and do your part in order to make things work.
5. Work as a team. Show interest in each other's interests.
6. Be open in your communications. Both parties should always be willing to talk freely.
7. Create a safe space where each partner can feel free to communicate their feelings without rejection or criticism.

8. Continue to cultivate love, respect, and understanding daily.
9. Make time for dates at least once per month.
10. Work at bringing passion to your relationship.
11. Be studious in financial management.
12. Learn to connect. Don't be pushy. Create intimacy.
13. Learn to share deep feelings.
14. Be monogamous.
15. Make trust a foundational principle in your marriage. Seek wisdom daily for positive enrichment in all the affairs of your relationships. Then, your marriage will flourish.

In conclusion, creating and developing closeness in marriage should be an ongoing process. People will continue to grow and change over time. Therefore, they must seek to understand the patterns of change that will occur as one grows individually.

Jesus lived the kind of life that He expects all of us to live. Let us try to live connected lives.

Building Marital Bonds

Dr. Trahern (Tron)

> "Many marriages would be better if the husband and the wife clearly understood that they are on the same side."
>
> — Zig Ziglar

Building a strong marital bond is one of the most important things a person can do in life. Building strong marital bonds is about commitment, trust, loyalty, and love. As a therapist, it's challenging when I see a marriage that was once composed of a team turn into opponents. Many years ago, I was counseling a couple. A disgruntled wife came into session, placed her husband in the center of the room, and said, "You need to fix him." This happened because, in a fit of rage, the husband shouted words of profanity towards the mother in front of the children. The wife was so hurt she could hardly look at her husband. Sadly, this mountain of unresolved feelings of resentment sunk the marriage. How could a husband utter such egregious words towards his wife? It was uncovered during sessions that there were built-up issues that happened in the beginning of the marriage that were unresolved. Can you imagine carrying baggage and weight for years? I have discovered when this baggage begins to implode, it will destroy the fabric of the relationship. So, at its core, this couple didn't start out well. As a side note, if you want to have a healthy relationship, I encourage you to get off to a good footing. This means selecting someone who has common core values and beliefs. This will safeguard against the many challenges that you will encounter in marriage. Sadly, this couple decided to sever their marital bond, which they were unwilling to rebuild and repair.

When resentments, hurts, and pains from the past become cemented in the foundation of the marriage, it is hard to break through. How do we avoid splitting the relational team? Two key components to safeguard a marriage are commitment and communication. When one is truly committed to their relationship, they're willing to work things out. Recently, I was counseling a couple that is seeking to build a healthy marriage. They had spent many years together, and now they were taking the next step. So, during our premarital counseling sessions, we discussed dreams, goals, and aspirations for the relationship. Then, we developed a mission statement for the marriage. I firmly believe that to have a healthy marriage, you need to have an end goal. One must identify where they would like to be, perhaps in a year, five, ten years, twenty years, or more from now. If you're considering building a relationship, maybe you need to sit down. As a pilot prepares for a flight, you need to check to ensure that everything is ready for the journey. But when there is a lack of commitment to the marital bond, it's hard to overcome difficulties. When the couple has one foot in and one foot out of the relationship, it's hard to overcome challenges if one has made up one's mind that the relationship is already over. Communication is important because when we fail to express our true feelings, it can turn into resentment over time.

Why do relationships that begin with joy end in sadness? While there are many reasons why this happens, I'm reminded of the scripture that says how can two walk together unless they agree? I often wonder why some couples spend thousands of dollars or more on weddings for everything to end later in heartbreak.

As a minister and counselor of marriage and families, my heart breaks to see the relationship bonds broken. When I perform wedding ceremonies, I hope the relationship will last. But the reality is statistically, almost 50% of marriages will end in divorce. So, what does it take to build bonds that nothing can separate? I believe it takes God at the center of a person's relationship and their lives individually to make relationships last. I have seen many things separate couples, such as ego, other people, and rigid mindsets. My hope is to provide tips on what can be done to overcome these pitfalls.

Here are some suggestions to help you strengthen your relational bond.

1. The secret of prayer. Couples should cultivate the habit of prayer together. This will be a safeguard against the distractions of this world. So, pray for each other daily. I recommend praying together at night before you go to sleep.
2. Understanding. It is important for individuals to understand each other's needs in marriage. I like to illustrate this by suggesting that everyone comes to the relationship with a shopping cart full of stuff. Whenever an individual goes into the shopping cart and tries to remove something, it can become a problem. Each person should be responsible for unloading their own shopping cart. So don't begin your next relationship by saying, "I'm going to change

this person by removing the items that are in their shopping cart."
3. Patience. It has been said that patience is a virtue. It's important that we remain calm under pressure. As we apply this practice, it helps us navigate our relationships more effectively.
4. Don't build up resentments and anger. When you feel tension arise, take a moment or two and express your frustrations in a helpful way.
5. Communicate about everything. Even when you don't feel like it, express your feelings.
6. Staying committed to one's vows helps during times of difficulties.
7. If there is a conflict, one must fight fair and not hit below the belt.
8. Be willing to make allowances for other people's faults. We must remember that our partner is not perfect, and neither are we.
9. Let go of the past and decide not to bring up faults once they have been worked through.
10. Schedule regular date nights. This provides an opportunity to reset your relationship goals.
11. Do not discuss your relationship with family, relatives, or friends. This is a quick way to strain your relational bond when you bring third parties into your relationships who don't have the training and skills to help you.
12. If you have a disagreement with your spouse, do not discuss it in front of the children.
13. Be an encourager in your relationship and not a discourager. Uplift your partner with your words.
14. If you encounter relational challenges, be willing to seek professional help to navigate them.

Chapter 10

Now What?

Pastor LaFavor

Developing a Blueprint for Your Relationships

What is a relationship blueprint? A blueprint is a detailed outline presenting a course of action. A blueprint in the counseling process helps clinicians be more effective in the counseling method.

Establish a blueprint for enhancing your relationship. A blueprint is essential to understanding how to build a relationship. You should continue to focus on good communication skills. Listen for what an individual is not saying, as well as what they are saying. Be patient with the ones that you are trying to bring along. This will help deliver exactly what is needed for the building process. When it comes to relationship building, all members must be urged to be honest, loyal, and supportive; if we do this, the relationship will grow. Spending time together encourages unity, empowers marriages, and helps form stronger bonds between siblings and extended family members.

Developing a blueprint for building strong relationships bonds. Building strong relationship bonds is important because they can be passed down from one generation to the next. Building powerful relationships bonds is concerned with sharing values, feelings, interests, ideas, and morals from past generations.

Build Relationships Bonds

So, what is the pathway for keeping the family together? We must search for the glue and good qualities that held past generations together. For example, my mother had four sisters, and my father had one sister. I personally witnessed the strong bonds that kept them loving and helping each other. I continue to practice those good values. I try to pass down those enduring principles to my children and grandchildren and all people who will listen.

What are the essential qualities for strengthening the foundation of family relationships? I believe that the key to building family bonds must be compelled by unconditional love. It means that love does not go away despite challenges or differences.

So, the answer to starting the task of building strong, meaningful relationships starts with oneself.

Firstly, we must discover who we are and decide what we want to do regarding relationship building. What is a blueprint for building strong bonds in family relations?

The goal is to formulate a plan for finding the means for bringing people together. It is good to come together and start to establish trust among members of the family. Find a way to create lasting bonds.

We must recognize that durable values are built on a foundation of communication, trust, honesty, hard work, forgiveness, and dedication.

Secondly, our focus must be on embracing the qualities that lead to restoration of the core principles of communication, commitment, commonality, dedication, and teamwork. Working together as a team will facilitate solving conflict and building family unity.

So, what is the meaning and value of relationship bonding? Proper family bonds are crucial to keeping good legacies alive. Let us get started in the process of developing closer family affiliations. Building strong relationships means developing a plan that demonstrates a guide for the enhancement of all our relationships.

Start a blueprint for awareness of better communication, commonality, understanding, and empathy. Communication is the foundational principle building block for strengthening bonds in relationships.

Communication is the exchange of thoughts, listening, sharing ideas, and information in an interpersonal relationship. Communication is extremely important in any relationship because it fosters understanding and helps us get through tough times. Positive communication helps bridge the gap and creates closeness in interpersonal relationships.

Trust is based on the degree of reliability and confidence in the faith that can be placed in the members of a group for the betterment and enrichment of the group.

Commitment refers to the dedication to the well-being, emotional and spiritual, and positive health of the partners of the members.

Commonality in shared values and similar upbringings provides a foundation for understanding family needs. Understanding each other contributes to promoting closeness in the family.

How do you build a stronger family relationship? We start the process of building bonds in the family system by devising a blueprint. A blueprint helps to target the areas of weak or strong personality traits in the family unit. Sometimes, we must go back and mend the brokenness that has happened in previous generations. Through communication and understanding, a way can be found to solve conflicts that exist in family systems.

Why do some siblings fight and call each other names and put-downs? Without support, these people have a difficult time accepting the changes. In the Western worldview, importance is currently placed on family closeness.

Another factor that has led to family disconnect is the gap in economic welfare and emotional awareness. A good resolution is to allow each sibling to feel the hurt before working out a solution.

Get them to hug and sit together for a moment. Remember that it will take effort, patience, and time to change unhealthy, toxic habits. Building strong relationships will require working together as a team, with the goal of creating lasting bonds.

What next? It is okay to speak to a competent family counselor about emotional issues in the nuclear and extended family connections. Jealousy and insecurity are the cause of division in many family circles.

What causes jealousy in family relationships? Jealousy in a family goes far back. It started soon after the creation of man. Envy feelings began in the human experience. Jealousy arises because of the arrival of the newcomers, who seem to be getting all the attention and gifts. Jealousy can also emerge from feelings of inadequacy; inferiority is a common cause of jealousy. Envy crops up in connections that result in family confusion.

A guide to relational reconciliation can come through members reaching out to each other with caring, encouraging words. According to the Bible, the greatest set of principles for bonding relationships can be found in the Book of Proverbs. Another way of creating closeness is by helping the disgruntled family members feel loved, valued, and needed.

Dr. Trahern (Tron)

Developing a Blueprint for Your Relationships

A blueprint is your roadmap to success. You can have the relationship that you have always desired, but it's going to take an action plan. We can reach our goals when we follow a constructive action plan. As a former professional athlete, I've learned that one must have a playbook or action plan. This plan should consist of your goals, desires, and dreams. The plan should consist of career, relational, financial, mental health, and spiritual goals.

Goals are important because they help us to stay on track when we face the inevitable challenges of life. It was action steps through a well-devised plan that helped me to pick up the pieces and rebuild after being released from the NFL. Zig Ziglar said you can't hit a target that you can't see. Perhaps we are aiming at the wrong target or running to the wrong place. It's not too late to embark upon the dreams you have always wanted.

But the key is to make the right choices. This means to stop making choices and decisions that do not serve your relationship well. My hope is *Rebuilding & Repairing Relationships* provides the ingredients to help you have the relationship you have always wanted. In this book, we sought to provide practical steps to deal with the challenges of life. We all face challenges, ups and downs, but the key is working through the difficulties to reach the end goal.

Why This Book Was Written

Pastor LaFavor

I have always been interested in how individuals interact and get along with each other. Family estrangement affects one in four people (*Psychology Today*). This book was written out of deep concern for the challenges and hardships faced in individual and family relationships.

Our aim in writing *Rebuilding & Repairing Relationships* is to provide a helpful handbook of wisdom to assist in healing and strengthening relationships. This was written based on years of spiritual and scientific experience. We hope the practical tools and resources we have provided help you overcome your relational challenges.

Why This Book Was Written

Dr. Trahern (Tron)

For over a decade, I have worked with individuals, couples, and families, helping them to repair, rebuild, and reestablish their relationships. We wrote this book out of care and concern for the challenges faced in relationships. Pastor LaFavor and I yearn to see families repaired, couples helped, and individuals inspired to achieve their goals in life. We hope the principles and insights this book shares can help enhance your relationships.

Reflections from Pastor LaFavor's Heart

Pastor LaFavor

I have had the wonderful honor of serving as the senior pastor of a Christian family-oriented church for over forty years. For over eighteen years, I have worked extensively with individuals struggling with severe mental health challenges. As a mental health therapist and chaplain, I was given the task of providing wisdom and insight to comfort clients during the most challenging seasons of their lives.

In *Rebuilding & Repairing Relationships*, I desired to use my education and experience to bridge the gap in relationships. I hope that individuals and families can experience closeness as they connect with the universal principles of sound health and well-being in this book.

This book is born out of my experience searching for workable methods for healing the gaps in my relationships. My hope is that as you read the chapters in this book, you find interventions and insights for bringing closeness to your relations.

I dedicate this book to the memory of my dear wife, Ellaree. For over half a century, we spent almost every day together. In our lifetime, we found the secret to repairing our relationship and dedicated our lives to helping others repair it.

Although my beloved departed to her eternal home in July of 2018, I am continuing our work. She was a beacon of light who faithfully brought many people to faith. May her memory always be cherished by all who knew of her work.

Dr. LaFavor's Reflections

It was truly a blessing to write this book with my father. For over fourteen years, I have worked extensively with him in the ministry to help empower the next generation for Christ. The spiritual foundation my father and mother, who is in heaven, provided me with has been instrumental in serving others. The tips and strategies in this book were born out of my experience as a son, counselor, and elder in the church. I understand life is filled with challenges and uncertainties. I have faced many obstacles on the road to rebuilding and dreaming again in my own life. Perhaps you are facing difficulties now. I hope *Rebuilding & Repairing Relationships* provides you with tools to help manage life's challenges. May this book serve as a guide to help you along your journey of life.

www.ingramcontent.com/pod-product-compliance
Lightning Source LLC
Chambersburg PA
CBHW070637160426
43194CB00009B/1484